World Karate Federation 3rd DAN Black Belt Recipient's

SHOTOKAN KARATE
EASIEST WAY TO GET BLACK BELT

DR. PRADEEP KUMAR YADAV

Clever Fox®
PUBLISHING

Chennai • Bangalore

CLEVER FOX PUBLISHING
Chennai, India

Published by CLEVER FOX PUBLISHING 2024
Copyright © Dr. Pradeep Kumar Yadav 2024

All Rights Reserved.
ISBN: 978-93-56488-67-0

This book has been published with all reasonable efforts taken to make the material error-free after the consent of the author. No part of this book shall be used, reproduced in any manner whatsoever without written permission from the author, except in the case of brief quotations embodied in critical articles and reviews.

The Author of this book is solely responsible and liable for its content including but not limited to the views, representations, descriptions, statements, information, opinions and references ["Content"]. The Content of this book shall not constitute or be construed or deemed to reflect the opinion or expression of the Publisher or Editor. Neither the Publisher nor Editor endorse or approve the Content of this book or guarantee the reliability, accuracy or completeness of the Content published herein and do not make any representations or warranties of any kind, express or implied, including but not limited to the implied warranties of merchantability, fitness for a particular purpose. The Publisher and Editor shall not be liable whatsoever for any errors, omissions, whether such errors or omissions result from negligence, accident, or any other cause or claims for loss or damages of any kind, including without limitation, indirect or consequential loss or damage arising out of use, inability to use, or about the reliability, accuracy or sufficiency of the information contained in this book.

FOREWORD

I have the honour of being the first woman in the world, to make history by winning six World Boxing Titles. My other accomplishments are Olympic Games Bronze Medal, Asian Games Gold Medal, Commonwealth Games Gold Medal. Furthermore, I have been conferred with the Padma-Vibhushan Award, the 2nd Highest Civilian Award granted in the republic of India.

I know Karate Coach Dr. Pradeep Kumar Yadav, as he is an official of the Rajya Sabha Secretariat, (Council of States) Parliament of India and I am the Member of Parliament, Rajya Sabha (Council of States), Republic of India. He has profound knowledge on Karate and for that; the world-wide renowned **"World Karate Federation, Spain"** has presented on him the Black Belt, 3rd DAN in Karate. He has exhibited his insight through this book where he has performed Karate positions with the depictions so that all Karateka can comprehend it in a simple manner. All photos are shaded with high-resolution. I think each Karateka should read this book as it covers full chapters from a White Belt to Black Belt in a straightforward way.

This book is extremely attractive in Paperback design and excellent paper quality. Its Coffee-Table size is appropriate to such an extent that everyone will fall in love with it at first sight. Further, it is worth reading this book because it not only tells about the method of achieving Black Belt very easily but justifies with its title too. Being a Boxer and an author of a book titled "Unbreakable"; I understand the significance of such an incredible and phenomenal reference book on Shotokan Karate.

I have perused this book and comprehend its significance in the present life as it helps bring in agility, strength and adaptability of the body and thereby ensuring overall wellbeing.

This book offers minutely analyzed and well demonstrated Karate stances; it will prove to be an expeditious source in acquisition of Black Belt in Shotokan Karate. I am extremely thrilled to recommend this tremendous, astounding, and wondrous book. Best of luck!!

(M.C. MARY KOM)
6 Time World Boxing Champion, Olympic Games Bronze Medalist,
Asian Games Gold Medalist, and Commonwealth Games Gold Medalist.
E-mail Id: mary.kom@sansad.nic.in

SHOTOKAN KARATE: EASIEST WAY TO GET BLACK BELT

किरेन रीजीजू
KIREN RIJIJU

D.O. No. 1435 MOS (HC)YA&S/20

राज्य मंत्री (स्वतंत्र प्रभार)
युवा कार्यक्रम एवं खेल मंत्रालय
और
राज्य मंत्री अल्पसंख्यक कार्य मंत्रालय
भारत सरकार
MINISTER OF STATE (I/C)
YOUTH AFFAIRS & SPORTS
AND
MINISTER OF STATE MINORITY AFFAIRS
GOVERNMENT OF INDIA

11 FEB 2020

MESSAGE

I am happy to know that your book "Shotokan Karate-Easiest Way to get Black Belt" is being published, which is based on your long experience in Karate Sports.

I am sure that this book will enhance knowledge and learning of the various skills of Karate Sports to young athletes. The book will also help the budding karate players to enhance their performance in the karate events. I hope you will continue to work for the development of karate with your skills and experience.

I congratulate you for publishing the book on Shotokan Karate sports.

(Kiren Rijiju)

Shri Pradeep Kumar Yadav,

401, 'सी' विंग, शास्त्री भवन, नई दिल्ली-110 001, दूरभाष : +91-11-2338 1185, 2338 6520, फैक्स : +91-11-2338 1898
401, 'C' Wing, Shastri Bhawan, New Delhi-110 001, Tel. : +91-11-2338 1185, 2338 6520, Fax : +91-11-2338 1898
11वां तल, पं. दीनदयाल अंत्योदय भवन, सी.जी.ओ. कॉम्पलेक्स, लोधी रोड, नई दिल्ली-110003, दूरभाष : +91-11-2436 4275
11th Floor, Pt. Deendayal Antyodaya Bhawan, C.G.O. Complex, Lodhi Road, New Delhi-110003, Tel. : +91-11-2436 4275

SHOTOKAN KARATE: EASIEST WAY TO GET BLACK BELT

*** TABLE OF THE CONTENTS ***

1. A. ABOUT THE AUTHOR..7
   B. INSPIRATION...8
   C. ACKNOWLEDGEMENTS...10
   D. WARNING..12
   E. GRATEFULNESS TO THE MENTORS..12
   F. PHOTO CREDITS...12
   G. COPYRIGHTS..13
   H. PREFACE..13
2. INTRODUCTION..15
3. HISTORY OF SHOTOKAN KARATE..17
4. EVOLUTION OF WORLD KARATE FEDERATION....................................38
5. BENEFITS OF SHOTOKAN KARATE..40
6. BASIS OF SHOTOKAN KARATE..46
7. PARAMETERS OF SHOTOKAN KATA...48
8. DEMEANOUR AND ATTITUDE DURING A COMPETITION........................50
9. SIGNIFICANT NOTES TO REMEMBER WHEN GRADING..........................51
10. SHOTOKAN KARATE PICTORIAL STANCES WITH DESCRIPTION................53
11. HONORARY RANKING IN SHOTOKAN KARATE....................................116
12. SHOTOKAN KARATE PERIOD FOR DAN GRADES................................118
13. LAYOUT OF KUMITE COMPETITION AREA......................................120
14. LAYOUT OF KATA COMPETITION AREA..122
15. SHOTOKAN KARATE KYU EXAMINATIONS......................................123
16. SHOTOKAN KARATE DAN GRADE EXAMINATIONS..............................134

17. REQUIREMENTS FOR A KYU GRADING IN SHOTOKAN KARATE……………136

18. POINT SYSTEM IN SHOTOKAN KARATE………………………………………..…….138

19. SPECIFICATIONS OF SHOTOKAN KATA BASSAI DAI……………………139

20. STEPWISE PROCEDURE OF SHOTOKAN KATA BASSAI DAI……………….141

21. SHOTOKAN KARATE TERMINOLOGY……………………………………………157

22. TWENTY PRINCIPLES OF SHOTOKAN KARATE………………………………...163

23. (A) SHARING RATIO OF BODY WEIGHT IN SHOTOKAN KARATE……………165

    (B) TARGET AREAS IN SHOTOKAN KARATE……………………………………...166

    (C) HANDS, FEET AND FISTS GLOSSARY IN SHOTOKAN KARATE……………166

    (D) COUNTINGS IN SHOTOKAN KARATE…………………………………………166

    (E) DIRECTIONS IN SHOTOKAN KARATE…………………………………………167

    (F) BLOCKS (UKE) IN SHOTOKAN KARATE………………………………………167

    (G) KICKS (GERI) IN SHOTOKAN KARATE………………………………………..168

    (H) PUNCHES (ZUKI) IN SHOTOKAN KARATE……………………………………168

    (I) STRIKES (UCHI) IN SHOTOKAN KARATE………………………………………169

24. INDEX……………………………………………………………………………………...169

25. BIBLIOGRAPHY……………………………………………………………………….171

SHOTOKAN KARATE: EASIEST WAY TO GET BLACK BELT

*** ABOUT THE AUTHOR ***

Postgraduate and born on 20/02/1978 in India, the author, Pradeep Kumar Yadav, started learning Karate from his schooldays in 1995 at Kendriya Vidyalaya No. 1, Delhi Cantonment, India. He got his 1st DAN Black Belt from the academy "Indo Shotokan Karate-do Federation, India" under the aegis of Shihan Balram Singh **6th DAN** Black Belt, who is the President, founder and Technical Director of this Federation. The author has a vast experience of training and coaching for more than 20 years. He received the Shodan Black Belt from the Karate Association of India, Ministry of Youth Affairs and Sports, Government of India. The author obtained the **3rd DAN** Black Belt in Karate as well in 2019 from the world renowned, **"World Karate Federation, Spain" (WKF).**

Established in 1990, the **World Karate Federation** is the largest international governing body of sports karate with 191 member countries. It is the only karate organization reorganized by the **International Olympic Committee,** with more than 10 million members worldwide. The International Olympic Committee is the supreme authority of sports that conducts the worldwide modern Olympic games movement, which is in Lausanne, Switzerland, created by Pierre de Coubertin and Demetrios Vikelas in the year **1894.** As of 2016, there are 206 National Olympic Committees worldwide, officially recognized by the International Olympic Committee. Indian Olympic Committee is also one of them.

Currently, The President of the World Karate Federation is Mr Antonio Espinos Ortueta. The headquarters of the World Karate Federation is in Madrid, Spain, and the styles recognized by the World Karate Federation are **Goju-Ryu, Shito-Ryu, Shotokan, and Wado-Ryu.**

The author is a Government Official of Rajya Sabha Secretariat, the Upper House, Parliament of India, that represents the largest electorate in the world.

To contact the Award-Winning Author and Karate Coach Dr. Pradeep Kumar Yadav, please visit his website at **www.pradeepkarate.com.**

*** INSPIRATION ***

My beautiful daughter Tanaya Yadav, a student of 7th class at DAV Public School, Sector-14, Gurugram, India, who has been honoured with the 8th KYU Yellow Belt in Shotokan Karate, was consistently the sole motivation to compose this book.

I dedicate this book to her. At some point, when she was taking Karate instructional course in Gurugram by Shihan Balram Singh, **6th DAN** Black Belt, I saw that the way she was doing both the Kumite and Kata was immediate and exact. She looks impressively assertive while performing Kumite and Kata in the class. Other coaches and students in the institute also acclaim her for her exceptional skills in the Shotokan Karate training class. My daughter asked me to write a book on Karate which stirred my heart and on that particular day, I assured myself that "Yes," I will write a book on Shotokan Karate with the goal that each Karateka should get the advantage through it regardless of any cost, spot, and time.

Therefore, after being decorated with the **3rd DAN** Black Belt from the **World Karate Federation, Spain,** I began writing this book enbedded with my High-Resolution pictures so that every Karateka should learn about the methods and movements of Shotokan style Karate in the most straightforward technique for comprehension. I have included every topic on Shotokan Karate that I learned from all my coaches for the past more than 20 years.

This book also has the merits of vision, inspiration, and motivation of "Khelo India School Games" movement launched on 31st January 2018 and "Fit India" movement launched on 29th August 2019 by the world's most popular and charismatic person, **Hon'ble Prime Minister of India, Shri Narendra Modi Ji** who asserted that the initiative is the need of the hour and will take the country towards a healthier future. The "Khelo India" program has been acquainted with restoring the game culture in India at the grassroots level by structuring a stable system for all games played in our nation and building up India as an athletically extraordinary country. In keeping with Hon'ble Prime-Minister Shri Narendra Modi Ji's vision, the **"Khelo India Movement"** and the **"Fit India Movement"** are expected to help young scout talent from the schools in various disciplines and groom them as future sports champions.

Launching of "**Fit India Movement**." Photo source: The Prime Minister's Office, India.

Launching of "**Khelo India School Games**." Photo source: The Prime Minister's Office, India.

*** ACKNOWLEDGEMENTS ***

I want to mention heartfelt thanks to my wife Sudesh Yadav, who is a Postgraduate Teacher in Chemistry at Kendriya Vidyalaya Sangathan, Ministry of Education, Government of India. I am grateful for all her help, patience, and support, without which I would not have been able to write this book. I am indebted to her for her generosity and selfless support in that she stood by my side during this project. If this book earns any praise, she deserves most of the credit.

I am appreciative of **Hon'ble Antonio Espinos Ortueta**, * who is the present President of both the **World Karate Federation** and the **European Karate Federation,** to believe in me all through and honouring me with **3rd DAN** Black Belt in Shotokan Karate. Former President of the Spanish Karate National Team and the Spanish Karate Federation, Mr Espinos, has headed the World Karate Federation since 1998 and the European Karate Federation since 1997. He is considered a significant power behind Karate's consideration in the program of the 2020 Summer Olympic Games in Tokyo.

I have great pleasure in acknowledging my gratitude to my Coach Shihan Balram Singh **6th DAN** Black Belt, who is also the President and founder of the academy "Indo Shotokan Karate-do Federation" in India, for his supportive nature and guidance. I shall eternally be grateful to him for his way of teaching Karate.

I am incredibly grateful to my senior coach Shihan Bharat Sharma **8th DAN** Black Belt whose creative approach towards traditional Shotokan Karate has been an inspiration for me. I would also thank him for his individual and organizational support and contributions to make me proficient in Shotokan Karate mastery. He has held the below positions also:

1. World Karate Federation Technical Commission Member.
2. President of South Asian Karate-do Federation for the session 2019-23.
3. Vice President of Delhi Olympic Association.
4. 1st Vice-President of Karate Association of India (Ministry of Youth Affairs and Sports, Government of India).
5. Executive Committee Member of the Asian Karate Federation.
6. Executive Member of the Asian Karate Federation.

SHOTOKAN KARATE: EASIEST WAY TO GET BLACK BELT

*** WARNING ***

The techniques depicted in this book and the strategies of any Shotokan Karate are perilous. You should, along these lines, train under the supervision and counsel of a certified coach. It will be ideal if you exercise self-control when rehearsing strategies portrayed in this book. Neither the writer nor the distributor of this book is liable for your preferred aftereffects to repeat these strategies independently; you do as such at your very own risk.

*** GRATEFULNESS TO THE MENTORS ***

The book "Shotokan Karate: Easiest way to get Black Belt" is reviewed by the expert Hanshi Bharat Sharma **8th DAN** Black Belt, who is also the Technical Commission Member of World Karate Federation. Hanshi Bharat Sharma has 45 years of training, teaching and coaching experience in traditional Karate. He has double-checked the accuracy of what you will learn here to ensure that this book gives you everything you need to know about Shotokan Karate.

*** PHOTO CREDITS ***

Photos Inside: Mr. Amit Dagar, Laxmi Photo Studio, Gurugram.

Cover Designer: Tanaya Yadav.

Cover Photo: Mr. Faizan, Kohli Printographics, Connaught Place, Delhi.

SHOTOKAN KARATE: EASIEST WAY TO GET BLACK BELT

*** COPYRIGHTS ***

All RIGHTS RESERVED. No part of this publication may be reproduced, distributed, or transmitted in any form by any means, including photocopying, recording, or other electronic, or mechanical methods, or any information storage and retrieval system, without the prior written permission of the author, except in the case of brief quotations embodied in critical reviews and certain other noncommercial uses permitted by copyright law. For permission requests, mail to the author, addressed "Attention: Seeking Permissions," at **pradeep7yadav@gmail.com.**

*** PREFACE ***

This book is composed for everyone who is inspired by the Shotokan Karate and needs to look behind credible Shotokan Karate more profoundly. For those, keen on extending their insight and improving their capacities with the applications depicted and delineated in this book, I recommend perusing this book completely to get each stance exhibited by me with their names along with full description about that particular stance so that it may be learned very well by the Karateka in a simple manner.

Why I am telling this is because true to this book's title, "Shotokan Karate: Easiest way to get Black Belt," every individual can comprehend it in the easiest way to achieve the Black Belt with the help of High-Resolution coloured photos. The best part of this magnificent book is its low cost and High-Resolution color photos, serving the goal that every single low-income family can bear to buy it and rest assured that it is gainful in learning Shotokan Karate most effortlessly.

SHOTOKAN KARATE: EASIEST WAY TO GET BLACK BELT

This book brings the entire knowledge of the Shotokan Kata from White Belt to Black Belt grade. At this crossroads, I might want to incorporate a short rundown of the most significant focuses that should be noted down when preparing and rehearsing the Kata techniques. Kata, the set down, conventional type of systems utilized against more than one aggressor, are the fundamental components of Karate. Each of the present elements of Karate originates from the Kata. To ace them, it requires a readiness to rehearse perpetually and as a prerequisite, to dive seriously into the subtleties described in the Karate book.

All the **High-Resolution colored photos** of every stances are mine, and I am playing out every one of Shotokan style Karate's stances in the right place. One ought not to mess with oneself with the deception that a Kata can be aced in a brief span. Numerous years are required to ace the movements of Karate and the various potential outcomes of utilizing them. What's more, this book incorporates a portrayal of the positions and subtleties of some advanced movements of the Shotokan style that are performed by me only. This book is precious and useful for those Karateka who need to take in Shotokan style Karate from White Belt to Black Belt with the aim of full devotion towards learning and rehearsing Karate. Each pursuer of this book will know much about the fundamentals of Shotokan Kata. Honestly, this book isn't just for novices; it is similarly helpful for cutting edge Karate trainees. This book makes Karate accessible to people of all ages, sexual orientations, and ranks.

Karate offers individuals of different ages the chance to learn authoritative aptitudes for self-defense with the capacity to dodge or escape strifeful experiences. Karate helps oneself to find, create, and keep up positive character attributes, like confidence, assurance, and perseverance. Karate encourages improvement in wellness, quality, and stamina, consequently helping one to improve their well-being and prosperity. Furthermore, every single hued photo in this book is mine, adorned with High Pixels of resolution, so that every Karate individual can see clear pictures and catch on it quickly in the mind in a simple manner.

As a Karate enthusiast and a recipient of 3rd DAN Black Belt in Karate from the acclaimed World Karate Federation, Spain, I have written this book "Shotokan Karate: Easiest Way to get Black Belt" solely for the promotion of Karate sport among the youth world-wide.

*** INTRODUCTION ***

Legendary Grandmaster Gichin Funakoshi, one of the world's most unique combative techniques Masters and educators, was the originator and inventor of Shotokan Karate-do, the most widely-known style of Karate, and is known as the **"Father of Modernistic and Contemporary Karate."**

Shotokan Karate-do is the most broadly refined Karate in the world. The other well-known hand-to-hand fights, such as Jujitsu, Judo, and Aikido, are performed in individual nations but not in all the countries. Karate, however, is by all accounts performed all over the world. As a technique for self-protection, Karate is unmatched. Its systems and applications are exact, unusual, snappy, and compelling. In any case, we accept that one of the fundamental explanations behind Karate's overall prominence is its natural openness. It tends to be rehearsed, for all intents and purposes, by any individual who appreciates healthy well-being, paying little mind to age or sex. You can do it in your way, and you can repeat it successfully, given that you are under the direction of a certified Coach or Sensei. I guarantee you will be on a safe Karate adventure.

SHOTOKAN KARATE LEGENDARY GRANDMASTER GICHIN FUNAKOSHI, JAPAN.

*** HISTORY OF SHOTOKAN KARATE ***

Bodhidharma was a Buddhist priest who is said to have been the transmitter of Zen (Chinese: Chan, Sanskrit: Dhyana, and English: meditation) to China. He was the third child of a Tamil king of the Pallava Dynasty. Bodhidharma is attributed with building up the acclaimed Shaolin School of Chinese Martial Arts which is referred to as Tripitaka Dharma Master. The records vary on the date of his appearance in China.

First, the book "**Anthology of the Patriarchal Hall**" describes that in 527, he visited Emperor Wu of Liang dynasty **(464-549)**. "Anthology of the Patriarchal Hall" narrates him as the 28th Patriarch of Buddhism also.

The second record is found in the book **"Further Biographies of Eminent Monks,"** where it proclaims that Bodhidharma arrived in China at the time of the Liu Song dynasty **(420-479)**.

BODHIDHARMA, AN INDIAN MONK. (The aforesaid photograph has been taken from www.mensxp.com and is being used as part of fair use. The copyrights and other intellectual rights of the said photograph belong to the respective right owners.)

His instructor, Prajnatara, changed his name from Bodhitara to Bodhidharma. On Prajnatara's death, Bodhidharma left his sanctuary in India to fulfil his teacher's last wish for going to China and spreading Buddhism. As per Chinese legends, he lived in a cave (near to shaolin temple and gazed at a wall for 9 years and didn't speak for the entire duration and cut his eye lids to get rid of sleep. Presently, this cave is known as **Bodhidharma cave.** Then, he entered at Shaolin temple to teach monks a series of external exercises which are known as the Eighteen Arhat Hands (Shi-ba Lohan Shou, and an internal practice which is called the Sinew Metamorphosis Classic. His birthday is celebrated on the 5th day of the 10th lunar month every year. The well-known Sanchin Kata, consolidated today in over twelve Okinawan karate styles, is frequently ascribed legitimately to Bodhidharma.

BODHIDHARMA CAVE NEAR SHAOLIN TEMPLE, CHINA. (The aforesaid photograph has been taken from www.onehandspeaks.com and is being used as part of fair use. The copyrights and other intellectual rights of the said photograph belong to the respective right owners.)

SHOTOKAN KARATE: EASIEST WAY TO GET BLACK BELT

This preparation strategy dependent on breathing systems and exposed knuckle or stick battling, spread later in China as **Kempo**. Bodhidharma wrote a book also, titled "**Ekkin-Kyo**," which is considered as the first book based on the martial art. Bodhidharma invented a preparation technique to build the priests mentally and physically healthy at **Shaolin temple**. The Shaolin Monks got known as the best contenders in China, and the method by which Bodhidharma instructed them was known as **Shaolin Kung Fu**. The Shaolin Monks went out of China to spread the fighting technology of Bodhidharma. Zen was promptly acknowledged in Japan.

SHAOLIN TEMPLE, CHINA. (The aforesaid photograph has been taken from www.flowingzen.com and is being used as part of fair use. The copyrights and other intellectual rights of the said photograph belong to the respective right owners.)

SHOTOKAN KARATE: EASIEST WAY TO GET BLACK BELT

One of the most ardent devotees of the Buddhist religion was Sho Shin. His father was King Sho En, ruler of Okinawa, and **Sho Shin** became the King of Okinawa in **1477** when he was 13 years old. He was a religious person and, therefore, banned the use of weapons. This boycott was continued by the Satsuma faction also. This prompted the underground improvement of striking techniques and may have empowered unarmed battle strategies intended for use against protected troopers, for example, Jiu-jitsu.

Okinawa was an independent nation controlled by the Ryukyu Kingdom and thrived through trade with China. Ryukyu turned into a prefecture of Japan because of the Abolition of the Han System that happened in **1879**. During the Pacific War, Okinawa was the primary site for fighting techniques in Japan that was open to a common man too. There were three martial arts branches, namely **Shuri-te** (Sokon Matsumura: 1828-1898) which were hard techniques by kempo with offensive play. Secondly, **Naha-te** (Kanryo Higaonna: 1853-1916) were softer techniques by Kempo with defensive plays through grappling, throws, and locks. Thirdly, **Tomari-te** (Kosaku Matsumora: 1829-1898) which were both soft and hard techniques of Kempo. These were named after the Okinawan towns inside which they were created. Shuri town was both political centre and capital. Naha town was a big seaport and trade centre. Tomari town was a smaller seaport. They were referred to by and large as Okinawa-Te or To-De. To-De, the hand to hand fighting of Okinawa could articulate as 'kara,' which means empty and 'Te' means hand, thus, Funakoshi named it as KARATE. In the long run, these formed into two mains styles, **Shorin-Ryu** that was created from Shuri and Tomari, was snappy and connected with natural breathing and was appropriate for physically light-build people. The other, **Shorei-Ryu** was originated from Naha which focused on constant, rooted motions with breathing synchronized with every movement and suitable for well-built people.

Karate was developed on the island of Okinawa, which lies in the south of the territory of Japan. After numerous years, the advancement of Karate as a method for self-protection increased in colossal ubiquity, as the Japanese government on the island had disallowed the utilization of weapons. Due to this national strategy, the self-protection procedures formed into an exciting Okinawan Karate specialty of "Karate" or **"void hand"** which involved only hand technique of combating at that time.

Karate is a hand technique right from its inceptions on the **Ryukyu Islands of Okinawa** in the East China Sea. The indigenous battling specialties of Okinawa were joined with hand-to-hand fighting of the neighboring nations, for example the White Crane style from Fujian, China. A significant number of the modern Karate styles began in Okinawa, which Japan used to administer. Okinawa is near "**Fuzhou**" a city in China. It is believed that combative techniques came to Okinawa through 'Fuzhou' by traders and tourists. As it is the traditional meeting point of Chinese and Japanese cultures, Okinawa became the place where the Okinawa Karate started to take shape in the mid-1800s and was known as '**Toudi**' (Tang Hand), China Hand or just Te (Hand). The most dedicated experts in Okinawa were individuals from the illustrious court in support of the Ryukyu lord. These pioneers of Karate were liable for keeping harmony and ensuring the safety of the imperial family, which generally tried their procedure. The coaching of Karate during this period was troublesome because of Japanese control on the Ryukyu kingdom, where the Japanese restricted the ownership of weapons and the act of Karate strategies. Therefore, Karate's work during this time was regularly led stealthily, around evening time, and in isolated territories. A significant number of the Kata we practice today were created or refined during this time.

SHOTOKAN KARATE: EASIEST WAY TO GET BLACK BELT

Legendary Grandmaster Gichin Funakoshi is generally viewed as the "Father" of modern Karate because of his endeavors to acquaint territory of Japan with the Okinawan Karate, from where it spread to the rest of the world. He was born on **November 10, 1868**, in Yamakawa, Shuri (Okinawa Prefecture). Being born into a family that had run into some bad luck implied that he spent his youth with his maternal grandparents. He started as a weakling, wiped out and in unexpected frailty, whose guardians carried him to Master Itosu for his karate preparation. His doctor, Tokashiki recommended certain herbs that would rejuvenate him. Soon Funakoshi got healthier. Master Gichin took coaching from **Yasutsune Itosu** in the initial stage of learning Karate. Funakoshi prepared with Azato stealthily since the Okinawans had their weapons prohibited and had to practice secretly. Master Funakoshi used to live in a small room with his students at **Suidobata,** Tokyo. He used to clean the dormitory during the day when the students were in their classes and take Karate classes at night. He made companion at school with the oldest child of the then-popular karate ace, Master Azato Anko and through this kinship, he was acquainted with Karate. His style of Karate started from him having prepared under two renowned Okinawan Karate experts, Master **Azato Anko** (1827-1906) and Master **Itosu Anko** (1831–1915). This art charted an impressive course of his life. He had become well-known in Ryukyu-style hand-to-hand fighting soon. As throughout the years he sought after his preparation and ceaselessly built up his wonderful aptitudes, Master Funakoshi accepted a job as an associate teacher at the primary school at the age of 20, in **1888**. He soon became Chairman of the Okinawa Martial Arts Society.

In 1898, karate was resolved to be no danger to the legislature and was permitted to be exhibited and rehearsed openly. Master Itosu is credited with encouraging the first Karate class at the Shurijijo Elementary School in Okinawa.

SHOTOKAN KARATE: EASIEST WAY TO GET BLACK BELT

In 1901, Karate training was legitimized in Okinawa, and its investigation got required in center schools. Being sure of consent from Azato and Itosu, Funakoshi declared that he would start officially educating Karate. Now he was 33 years old.

In 1902, when **Shintaro Ogawa**, the Commissioner of school education in the Kagoshima Prefecture, having seen a presentation of Karate given by Master Funakoshi, presented a report to the Ministry of Education in Japan about the advantages of the preparation in karate, Karate turned into a part of the educational plan in schools and started to be polished uninhibitedly in Japan.

In 1916, the historical Shotokan karate really started with Master Gichin Funakoshi's trip to Kyoto, where karate was shown without precedent for Japan, at the Butokuden. While the showing was effective and the Japanese were highly intrigued, there was no prompt race to carry the Okinawan art to Japan on a conventional premise. Although impressed with it, the Japanese, despite everything, would in general be dubious of anything simply Okinawan, and they thought that it was convenient to see karate as a fascinating sideshow. This mentality could have been the end of karate in Japan had it not been for a serendipitous occasion on **March 6,1921**. On that day, the Crown Prince (the Emperor Hirohito of Japan visited Okinawa while on his visit to Europe. Looking to impress the Prince with the rich culture of Okinawa, the Department of Education asked Funakoshi to give a karate show for him in the **Great Hall of Shuri Castle, Okinawa, Japan.** So entranced was the ruler by the exhibition that he talked about it enthusiastically all through the remainder of his journey. In this manner the Ministry of Education officially mentioned a karate show be performed at the main National Athletic Exhibition in Tokyo. Funakoshi was obviously picked to perform. It made a strong positive impression on the Japanese public also. The Japanese government appreciated this new way. From that point onwards, Karate turned out to be exceptionally prevalent and spread quickly in Japan. During

Funakoshi's exhibition, he had made his Karate enthusiasts be dressed in a similar Gi as the Judo students do; at that point, he put the belts on them and had them show significant accomplishments. He renamed the technique from "To-Te Jutsu" (the method of the Chinese hand) to "Karate-do" (the technique for the Empty Hand).

SHURI CASTLE, NAHA, OKINAWA, JAPAN. (Photo by CEphoto, Uwe Aranas. The aforesaid photograph has been taken from www.commons.wikimedia.org and is being used as part of fair use. The copyrights and other intellectual rights of the said photograph belong to the respective right owners.)

He spread the specialty of Karate-do with endless enthusiasm, and this made him considerably fruitful. Now, Funakoshi turned into an exceptionally well-educated Master. Funakoshi additionally functioned as a calligraphist and creator, expanding his works under the pen name of "**Shoto**." He was notable in Japan and progressively found new Karate adherents from various colleges.

In 1922, at the age of 54, he presented Okinawan Karate-Jutsu before the Ministry of Education, Japan. This presentation, the first-ever open showcase of Karate-Jutsu in Japan, was a dazzling achievement. Promptly, the founder of Judo, **Master Jigoro Kano** and his student,

Gima Shinkin, welcomed Master Funakoshi to give a presentation of Kata. Remarkably, Master Funakoshi was requested from all sides to remain in Tokyo. Energized by the chance to further advance the Karate that he had accomplished to such a great deal, in Japan, Master Funakoshi started showing it at Tokyo's Meiseijuku quarters for Okinawan. Here, it is important to emphasize that Master **Jigoro Kano** was the only man who invented **Judo-gi** which was derived from the **KIMONO** dress, a Japanese traditional garment and later Master Funakoshi adopted and invented new **Karate-gi** which was lighter in weight than Judo-gi. In 1922, Funakoshi published a book entitled **"Ryukyu Kempo: Karate,"** which has the honor of being the first-ever book in the history of Karate and quickly made an exceptional Karate success.

KIMONO DRESS WORN BY A JAPANESE WOMAN. (The aforesaid photograph has been taken from www.yoycart.com and is being used as part of fair use. The copyrights and other intellectual rights of the said photograph belong to the respective right owners.)

The emblem for Shotokan Karate, **"The tiger in the circle" or "Tora no maki" or "The tiger roll,"** was planned by the well-known artist **Hoan Kosugi** (December 30, 1881- April 16, 1964), a companion of Master Funakoshi, to represent his books about Karate. The emblem is generally utilized and received all-inclusively by Shotokan Karate club affiliations till now. Respectfulness, regard, and the protective qualities of Karate, which were secured as the fundamental topics in Funakoshi's standards, are altogether symbolized in the logo of Shotokan Karate. The tiger in the circle outlines the rules of Karate-do. The tiger represents the capacity to battle and win, yet the limits of the circle constrain its opportunity and forcefulness. The ring speaks of tolerance, though, sensibility, knowledge and control are the core of Karate-do.

SHOTOKAN EMBLEM

ARTIST HOAN KOSUGI

World War-II during 1939-1945, unleashed destruction on the whole world and the Karate world was specifically affected badly. Precious records of the history and legacy of Karate were lost during the attack on Okinawa; many Japanese Karatekas lost their lives attempting to safeguard their nation.

In 1922, Master Gichin Funakoshi, acquainted the people of Japan more with Karate during the 1st National Athletic Exhibition held in Tokyo. The exhibition ended up being an extraordinary accomplishment because of the rising fame of Master Funakoshi. He showed just a single strategy, a complete discipline, which spoke to a blend of Okinawan styles. This strategy was known as Shotokan.

Shotokan incorporates Kanji symbols in the Japanese language as **SHOTO-KAN**, which was picked by Funakoshi's students to name his first close-to-home dojo, and it gets its name from his pseudonym, **'Shoto,'** signifying **'Pine Waves,'** and **'Kan,'** which means **'House,'**.

In 1924, Funakoshi was requested by Professor Shinyo Kasuya of the German Language Department to teach Karate at **Keio University**. The Keio University authorities were so impressed by the teachings of Master Funakoshi that they established the Karate-do Club at Keio University. Later, many Japanese Universities had Karate clubs where research of Karate used to be conducted that brought Karate to the modern era. The Keio, Waseda, Hosei, and Takushoku represent the top Karate colleges in Japan, with the highest social and political status. As the prevalence of Karate-Jutsu started to spread, Master Funakoshi created the first-ever **"DAN Ranking Certification"** in April 1924. During this period, Funakoshi and his son Yoshitaka or Gigo Funakoshi included Kumite (battling techniques), the Japanese KYU/DAN Ranking System, and a portion of the conventional ideas of Budo (Martial Way to the art). Around the same time, with the support of his instructor of Buddhism, **Abbot Furukawa Gyodo** (1872-1961) of Engakuji Temple in Kamakura, Master Funakoshi began rehearsing Zen. He was requested to advance the Okinawan Karate in the rest of Japan. Master Funakoshi blended a total arrangement of techniques and hypotheses and changed the Chinese and Okinawan names of the Kata into standard Japanese.

In 1929, after much ideation and reflection, he additionally changed the name of Karate-Jutsu (Chinese-hand Karate technique) to Karate-do (the method for Karate, or the way for the empty hand). He, at that point, characterized the **"Twenty precepts of Karate"** and built a fantastic Karate reasoning. Finally, the method for Karate had made its mark and was picking up ubiquity the whole way across Japan.

KEIO UNIVERSITY, JAPAN. (Photo by Kakidai-own work. The aforesaid photograph has been taken from www.commons.wikimedia.org and is being used as part of fair use. The copyrights and other intellectual rights of the said photograph belong to the respective right owners.

In 1930, Funakoshi further expanded Karate studies in Japan. The colleges were the significant destinations of Karate study, and they were impacted by research on physiology and workout. Under Yoshitaka, the improvement of Shotokan Karate truly quickened that brought straightforwardness in the intensity of punching and kicking methods. This learning consolidated into the Kihon (basics) of Shotokan Karate. During the 1930s, Karate's further styles, Goju-Ryu, Shito-Ryu, and Wado-Ryu, had been created notwithstanding the form of Shotokan Karate. These styles were additionally presented by Masters from Okinawa, which are as follows:

1. Shito-Ryu (Japan), which was established by Master Kenwa Mabuni in 1928, and was based on practicing a lot of Kata to bring out perfection instances.

2. Goju-Ryu (Okinawa), which was formed by Master Chojun Miyagi in 1930, and was based on using circular block and Jujitsu techniques.

3. Shoto-Ryu (Japan), which was defined by Master Gichin Funakoshi in 1938, and was based on doing wide stances that deliver powerful attacks rapidly on an opponent.

4. Wado-Ryu (Japan), which was created by Master Hironori Otsuka in 1939, and was based on a natural posture to dodge the assailant's attack or to make it minimize.

On January 29, 1936, the first official Shotokan Dojo "Dai-Nihon Karate-do Shoto-Kan" was opened in Zoshigaya, Mejiro, Tokyo. Japanese Karate-ka contributed funds to manufacture the main building of Karate dojo, which they named Shotokan in regard of Funakoshi Sensei. Unfortunately, it was demolished by an allied forces' air attack on April 29, 1945. Under Master Funakoshi, the first Shihans (Senior teachers) were **Takeshi Shimoda** (1901-1934), Master's first remarkable student, who died in 1934 at a young age and **Yoshitaka Funakoshi** (1906-1945) who died young in 1945. The number of individuals wishing to start practice was increasing day by day. The Katas modified to adjust to a dynamic new style. After being seen by the Japanese Ministry of Education during a Karate exhibit, Funakoshi approached it to carry his Karate to colleges in Japan for guidance. His presentation of the Karate technique was successful there and he sent forward an assortment of extraordinary students, like Takagi and Nakayama of Nippon Karate Kyokai, **Yoshida** of Takudai, **Obata** of Keio, **Noguchi** of Waseda, and Otsuka, the organizer of Wado-Ryu karate to different colleges and universities in some territories of Japan.

After the 2nd World War residue settled **in 1945,** one of Master Funakoshi's top students, Masatoshi Nakayama started to sort out the rest of the students and recoup the lost preparing strategies of Kata and Kumite. Gichin Funakoshi assumed a significant job in acquainting Japan with karate from Okinawa, acclimated to decrease injury and converged with approaches for athletic preparation. There were some senior students of Master Funakoshi including **Masatoshi Nakayama**, **Isao Obata,** and **Hidetaka Nishiyama** who wanted to form an organization which would be dedicated to the promotion, education, management and research of Karate. Therefore, on **May 27, 1949** an organization was formed which is known as **Nihon Karate Kyokai or Japan Karate Association (JKA).** This organization was totally dedicated to Master Funakoshi's endeavors. Master Funakoshi was appointed as the supreme commander of the JKA and Hidetaka Nishiyama was appointed as the Chief Instructor. The Japan Karate Association (JKA) started framing rules for Karate challenges, including a focus on Kata and Kumite. These rivalries aligned Karate closer with different indigenous Japanese hand-to-hand fights, for example, kendo and judo. Today, Karate-do is spread over several nations around the globe. He needed to clarify that the essential tutoring and preparation must be the significant prime point. At this point, Master Funakoshi had, for quite some time, been instructing Karate to secondary school and college students. Subsequently, Karate clubs had jumped up at advanced education foundations all over Japan, which is another motivation behind why Karate has moved towards being regarded as it is today.

In May 1949, a few of the first Shotokan Karate Masters split from the JKA association. One of these was **Hirokazu Kanazawa** (May 3, 1931 – December 8, 2019, known as "**Kancho**." Kanazawa was the protege of the late superintendent of the Shotokan style, Masatoshi Nakayama, and was one of the only a handful few outstanding Karate experts who contemplated under Master Gichin Funakoshi himself.

SHOTOKAN KARATE: EASIEST WAY TO GET BLACK BELT

On April 10, 1957, the Ministry of Education, Japan, gave legal recognition to the JKA, turning it into a rightful institute. After sixteen days past this recognition, Master Funakoshi passed away on **April 26, 1957** at the age of 89. An enormous open remembrance was held at the Ryogoku Kokugikan (Ryogoku National Sumo Hall, which included 20,000 individuals, including numerous sports celebrities and government officials that came to offer their tribute. A commemoration landmark to Master Funakoshi was built up at **Engakuji Temple in Kamakura, Japan. On April 29,** every year, the date of the Shoto Festival, individuals from the JKA pay a privileged visit to this memorial. A commemoration to Gichin Funakoshi was raised by the Shotokai at Engakuji, a monastery in Kamakura, on December 1, 1968. Designed by **Kenji Ogata** the landmark highlights calligraphy by Funakoshi and **Sogen Asahina** (1891–1979, the main priest of the monastery which bears the words **"Karate ni sente nashi,"** which means **"There is no first attack in Karate."**

GRANDMASTER GICHIN FUNAKOSHI MEMORIAL AT ENGAKUJI TEMPLE, KAMAKURA, JAPAN. (The aforesaid photograph has been taken from www.deviantart.com and is beingused as part of fair use. The copyrights and other intellectual rights of the said photograph belong to the respective right owners.

The JKA had already started its well-known educator training project and started to create the absolute, most capable, gifted, and formidable Karate specialists on the planet. Ace Nakayama utilized the educator course to spread the humble Okinawan Karate worldwide. Remarkable educators from the JKA instructional classes included Masters **Hidetaka Nishiyama** (October 10, 1928 – November 7, 2008), **Teruyuki Okazaki** (June 22, 1931 – April 21, 2020), **Yutaka Yaguchi** (November 14, 1932), **Hirokazu Kanazawa** (May 3, 1931 – December 8, 2019), **Keinosuke Enoeda** (July 4, 1935 – March 29, 2003), **Takayuki Mikami** (January 1, 1933), **Tetsuhiko Asai** (June 7, 1935 – August 15, 2006), and numerous others. These incredible educators formed the universe of Karate work during the height of its ubiquity during the 1960s and 1970s.

During the 1st Japanese Master's Championship in 1957, as indicated in the reports by the JKA Instructor Teruyuki Okazaki, he was providing guidance in the Central Dojo of the JKA consistently, straight up to a couple of days before his death. The JKA proceeded with the spreading of Shotokan Karate with Funakoshi's point, with overall accomplishment under the initiative of Masatoshi Nakayama. Nakayama set down the required measures for the procedures, groupings, and use of the Shotokan Kata in his books, which are followed till now.

ENGAKUJI TEMPLE, KAMAKURA, JAPAN. (Photo by Andrea Schaffer from Sydney, Australia. The aforesaid photograph has been taken from www.commons.wikimedia.org and is being used as part of fair use. The copyrights and other intellectual rights of the said photograph belong to the respective right owners.)

The 1st JKA All Japan Karate Championship was held in **October 1957** in Tokyo. When this yearly competition's framework was setting up, it wasn't long before there were many JKA karate branches in towns, schools, and renowned colleges in Japan. **In 1958,** Master Nakayama was delegated as the Chief Instructor. **In 1961,** His Majesty, the Crown Prince of Japan (presently His Majesty the Emperor of Japan), went to attend the fifth JKA All Japan Karate Championship. The JKA karate had become noticeable. This period saw dynamic advancement in the art of Karate. As a consequence of consistent coaching among educators, the complete framework of Karate was formed. For the first time, the best forms for each Kumite position, stance, and action merged in a proper scientific way. There was a clear distinction between the "correct" and "incorrect" approach to execute every technique, position, punch, and kick. When these methods were created, several teachers went abroad to spread Karate's specialty around the globe. The JKA was the principal karate association to set up dojo outside Japan. That's why the JKA is so famous and influential in the world. During this period, the JKA further built up its karate guidance framework and keeping in mind the incredible growth of its branch dojo all through Japan, it started sending some of its most exceptionally trained, proficient educators to America, Europe, and the Middle East to instruct and build up the dojo. Karate was turning into success outside Japan as well. Moreover, the JKA turned into the leading karate association to send its certified full-time educators to demonstrate Karate in colleges. Ace Teruyuki Okazaki and Hidetaka Nishiyama (October 10, 1928 – November 7, 2008), were instructed by the JKA in 1961, to spread Shotokan Karate in the USA.

In 1975, by acknowledging Karate's entry into the Olympics as a top priority, the first universal competition supported by the JKA, the IAKF (International Amateur Karate Federation) World Cup was held in the U.S., and it continued for the three more times later also. Notwithstanding, to safeguard the whole system and soul of Ippon-Shobu (bringing down the adversary with one blow), the JKA organized another competition, the first-ever worldwide Shoto World Cup Karate Championship Tournament in 1985 and that was a declaration of how much global a martial technique Karate had become.

In 1977, Ace Okazaki built up the **"International Shotokan Karate Federation" (ISKF)** in Philadelphia which was assigned the overall central command. The ISKF ceaselessly developed and thrived as a part of the Japan Karate Association (JKA until 2007), setting up an Instructor Training Institute in the USA to reflect the JKA training program.

In 1978, Hirokazu Kanazawa (1931–2019), 10th Dan, split away from the JKA and formed **Shotokan Karate-do International Federation (SKIF).** Kanazawa had trained under Masatoshi Nakayama and Hidetaka Nishiyama who were the two students of legend Gichin Funakoshi. SKIF presented components of TAI-CHI, especially in the matter of balance, and effectively advanced the development of Shotokan art. Kanazawa is viewed as one of the most splendid Shotokan master. Most prominently, he won the kumite title at the main JKA Open Tournament (in 1957 with a wrecked hand). Kanazawa was granted 10th Dan in 2000. Established in **October, 1978** with over two million individuals in 103 nations around the world, the SKIF is the world's most prominent Shotokan Karate association. Shotokan Karate is one of the most prevalent of the present-day styles. It is the most dominant and dynamic of Japanese techniques. In his late 70's, Master Hirokazu Kanazawa was the Chairman and Chief Instructor of the Shotokan Karate-do International Federation (SKIF) and was holding the evaluation of 10th DAN.

Master Masatoshi Nakayama (April 13, 1913 – April 15, 1987), who became the second Chief Instructor of the JKA after Sensei Funakoshi died in November 1957, was the only man to spread Karate worldwide in the **1960s and 1970s** and put it on a scientific method through Kinesiology, Anatomy, Psychology, and Physics associated with Karate techniques. He had started learning Karate under the incredible ace Gichin Funakoshi in 1931. After moving on from Takushoko University in 1937, he had gone to Peking to learn the Chinese language, where he also examined different styles of Chinese fighting techniques there. He also published various books, including "Dynamic Karate," a top to bottom scientific method of Kihon, and several videos of specialized and pragmatic data on Kata, Kihon, and Kumite. Sensei Masatoshi Nakayama held the position of 10th Dan at the age of 74. When Master Nakayama died, the JKA suffered disturbances, continuing for two decades.

In 1986, Nobuyuki Nakahara (Born on December 11, 1934), a recognized business tycoon and former Tokyo University Karate Club partner, was delegated as the 8th Chairman of the JKA. Japan Karate Association (JKA) is a top and reputed Karate organization at the international level. Masters who represent the JKA Shotokan Karate at a global scale, are **Taiji Kase** (February 9, 1929 – November 24, 2004) from the European branch in Paris, **Hideki Ochi** in Germany, **Hiroshi Shirai** in Italy, **Keinosuke Enoeda** (July 4, 1935 – March 29, 2003) in Great Britain, **Satoshi Miyazaki** (June 17, 1938 – May 31, 1993) in Belgium, **Higashino** in Brazil, **Ishiyama** in Venezuela, **Stan Schmidt** (the first non-Japanese fifth dan in South Africa, **Hideki Okamoto** (July 30, 1941– April 30, 2009) in Syria and Lebanon, **Masahiko Tanaka** (born on February 24, 1941) in Denmark, **Sasaki** in the Philippines, **Hiroshi Matsuura** in Mexico, and others. Around 5,000,000 individuals currently rehearse the JKA Shotokan karate-do in almost every nation in the world. The command of the JKA is to add to world harmony by directing exploration and giving Karate-do guidance. It aims at affecting youngsters and teenagers to improve their physical and emotional well-being just as developing the soul of combative techniques and the idea of Japanese martial art which highlights behaviour and honour.

In 1990, the official status of the JKA was in a crisis when a few of its segregated members unlawfully changed the executive register. It faced a massive disaster for a long time. The Japan Supreme Court rejected these separated members' appeal in **June 1999** and closed the case forever. During this period, the JKA continued its progress under the instructions of the Chief Instructor Master **Sugiura Motokuni** (October 4, 1924 – August 10, 2015). With its lawful status re-established by court decisions, the JKA jumped into the 21st Century. It re-built its interior association and revamped its monetary base. **In December 2000,** it bought land and set up its new central command and dojo in the centre of Tokyo. The fantastic opening function was held in **May 2001,** by various dignitaries and numerous individuals from other karate associations. With recharged power, the JKA repositioned itself, plainly characterizing itself as "**The Keeper of Karate's Highest Tradition.**" **In 2004,** the JKA introduced an official website, through which it proceeds, as usual, to advance genuine Karate around the globe.

On March 21, 2012, through consistent obligation and its responsibility to the community, the JKA was additionally distinguished by the legislature of Japan as KOEKI SHADAN HOJIN (open intrigue joined relationship). The JKA is the leading Japanese combative techniques relationship till date to be given such an acknowledgment by its government.

On April 7, 2020, Chairman of Japan Karate Association, Kusahara Katsuhide, announced postponement of the Gichin Funakoshi Cup due to the spread of the Covid-19 globally.

*** EVOLUTION OF WORLD KARATE FEDERATION ***

Karate was demonstrated for the first time in Europe around the **1950s** by the Japanese masters, particularly from the Japan Karate Association. In **1961,** Jacques Delcourt was designated the President of French Karate Federation, which was at that stage an affiliated member of the French Judo Federation. In **1963,** he requested the six other known European federations like Great Britain, Belgium, Italy, Germany, Spain, and Switzerland to come to France for the first-ever international karate event, wherein Great Britain and Belgium agreed for the proposal.

In December **1963,** six of the seven federations assembled in Paris for the first European Karate conference. The aim was to improve and organize karate tournaments among their countries. It was noted that the unification of the different karate styles was impossible. So, in **1965,** the European Karate Union was established and Jacques Delcourt was elected as President. In **1966,** the 1st edition of European Karate Championships was held in Paris, France from 7th May to 9th May. The contest attracted around 300 spectators and was displayed on live TV. Nevertheless, it drew criticisms for being too brutal as there were many facial injuries of the Karatekas. However, the EKU council had different opinions about the source of the injuries. The EKU observed that excessive violations of rules may be the reason for injuries. This problem was taken into consideration in the 1st referee course, held in Rome. Thereby, for the first time, the JKA rules were implemented in refereeing rules.

In **1970,** Jacques Delcourt constituted the International Karate Union (IKU) to show Karate at the world level. This information came in the knowledge of Ryoichi Sasakawa, who was the President of the Federation of All Japan Karatedo Organization (FAJKO), which later modified its name to the Japan Karate Federation (JKF). He went to France to explore the establishment of an international governing body. Ryoichi Sasakawa, President of the Japan Karate Federation (JKF) and Jacques Delcourt, President of the European Karate Union (EKU) mutually proposed a progression of gatherings that would deliver not just the main amalgamated worldwide principles for sport Karate, yet in addition the foundation of the World Union of Karate Do Organizations **(WUKO)** on **October 10, 1970.** 1st WUKO world championship was held at Tokyo in 1970 with 33 countries as participants. Here, the achievement, scale and media effect of the occasion was quickly perceived worldwide as an inventive achievement in the advancement of game Karate.

In **1985,** the World Union of Karate-do Organizations was authoritatively acknowledged by the International Olympic Committee as the legal board for karate. WUKO tried to incorporate with the International Traditional Karate Federation (ITKF) founded by Hidetaka Nishiyama in 1990 to form the WKF. However, this attempt failed and the WUKO group left to form the WKF on their own. In the early **1990s,** Hidetaka Nishiyama's refusal to align his ITKF organization with the World Union of Karate-Do Organizations (WUKO) caused the International Olympic Committee to suspend its recognition of WUKO as amateur karate's international governing body.

The reconciliation of a few new associations during the 1990s saw WUKO enrollment increment to 150 National Federations. In this manner, another name that would, all the more precisely, mirror the size and extent of the association was required. Hence, on **December 20, 1992,** the name of the International symbolizing Karate was hence changed to World Karate Federation (WKF). **17th June** is the World Karate Day declared by the World Karate federation in **2017**.

*** BENEFITS OF SHOTOKAN KARATE ***

A. YOU WILL PROTECT YOURSELF:

Like different kinds of martial art, Karate training gives you strategies that could save your life if the circumstance emerges. Karate sets you up to guard yourself against aggressors by giving you the faculties to respond rapidly and viably in dangerous conditions. Karate is such an all-encompassing technique that if you face any assailant, you are sufficient to defeat them in that situation. So, in this way you are prepared to fight in such an odd situation during day or night. If such situation occurs in the crowd and you defeat the attacker, then obviously, you will not only earn appreciation by the people at site, it will boost your self-confidence and self-image. Simply, the more you practice, the healthier you will get to face such emergencies.

B. FITNESS BENEFITS OF KARATE:

1. COMPLETE BODY WORKOUT: Nearly considered as a wellness and health improvement plan, Karate gives a full-body exercise that focuses on enhancements in cardiovascular capabilities and endurance. There's no denying that Karate is outstanding among other absolute body exercises. It consolidates cardio, aerobic exercise, and muscle conditioning while at the same time-consuming unnecessary fat.

2. STRENGTHENS CARDIOVASCULAR SYSTEM: One of the most noteworthy advantages of Karate is its positive impact on your cardiovascular framework. Karate activities will improve the heart's capacity to pump the blood to every part of our body and thereby improving your heart's well-being. It maintains healthy heart rate and well-regulated your oxygen intake.

3. ENHANCES MUSCLE TONING: By taking part in Karate, you can tone the body fat you have in your body. Karate preparation will reinforce and pretty much strengthen every muscle in your body. Trust me. Doing bunches of pushups, abs, and preparing positions like the Kiba Dachi or the Zenkutsu Dachi will assist you in increasing a few muscle masses, which will prompt an expansion in your general deftness.

4. INCREASES STRENGTH AND POWER: Karateka regularly practice activities, for example, pushups, crunches, and an assortment of other body-weight exercises intended to advance expanded muscle strength. Yet it is their preparation of strikes that delivers benefits over the long haul.

5. INCREASES MUSCLE COORDINATION: The most particular and useful part of reliable preparation in any hand to hand fighting style is its impact on coordination and muscular correspondence. As you develop in understanding, an ever-increasing number of movements and procedures will require and create more prominent general coordination just as deftness. Research has exhibited that by rehearsing Karate, you not only permanently improve your reflexes in the Karate but in everyday activities like driving also.

6. ENRICHES STAMINA AND ENDURANCE: Continuous Karate rehearsing will help increment of endurance in your entire body and will improve your breathing capacities. Within half a month, you'll understand how harder and progressively safe you are. You'll have the option to last more and feel less tired during preparation. Expanding your endurance is fundamental for a healthy life as it can steady your pulse, blood pressure, and help consume fat.

7. HEIGHTENS FLEXIBILITY: Stretching, kicking, and other Karate movement will assist with expanding muscle and joint adaptability so you can do different stances, activities, and movements better in life. If you continue stretching excercises, you will see progressive and considerable improvement after some time.

8. ENHANCES AGILITY: Through the act of different Karate works out, you will build up the capacity to be quick in response movements. You'll be surprised at how quickly your feet will execute entangled footwork.

9. INCREASES BALANCE AND MOBILITY: Regular practice of Karate kicks, Kata, and Kihon are the extraordinary methods in improving the body balance.

10. IMPROVEMENT IN SCHOOL ACADEMICS PERFORMANCE: Every Karateka will perform well in academics or in any office due to the rising level of energy, focus, and concentration that he or she achieves during the Karate practice.

C. HEALTH BENEFITS OF KARATE:

1. IMPROVE WEIGHT LOSS: You will utilize your hands, feet, elbows, and knees, and each strike will connect with your abdominal muscle strength and offer a brilliant full-body exercise. By and large, a one-hour moderate power Karate class can reduce upto 500 calories and specific fighting class, you can kill upto 1000 calories during a one-hour session. You will notice that undesired fat breaks down.

2. ENHANCES STABILITY & POSTURE: Abdominal muscle is required when performing punches or kicks, squares, and even avoidance and evades. The outcome will be a general better body stance and posture.

3. REGULATES GLUCOSE AND INSULIN LEVELS: Exhausting physical exercise assists in maintaining sugar control. Karate practice makes your heart beat quicker. Your muscles utilize more glucose. After some time, this can bring down your glucose levels. It additionally makes the insulin in your body.

4. REDUCES SYSTEMIC INFLAMMATION: Abundance of insulin and blood sugar is provocative to the body. So, the more you practice, it will reduce overall body inflammation by controlling your insulin and glucose levels.

5. MELTS AWAY STUBBORN BODY FAT: Karate invigorates the hormonal level, which assists in continuing fat-consumption considerably even after your training sessions.

6. MUSCLE TONE: Conditioning your muscles lessens fat and body weight. Weight reduction from the body brings about an improvement in wellbeing, which benefits the heart, joints and skeletal framework. A conditioned body gives more quality, vitality and adaptability, and can diminish the danger of building up specific sicknesses, for example, diabetes and coronary illness. This can be done through Karate.

7. ENHANCES SLEEP QUALITY: Making Karate a vital part of your week's program will add to a more beneficial, progressively peaceful, and continuous rest.

8. IMPROVES HEART RATE AND BLOOD PRESSURE: Rehearsing Karate that includes quick and movements at high speed requires a degree of wellness that will ultimately assist in healthy pulse rate.

9. RELIEVES STRESS: Karate's preparation runs on profound breathing activities, like the strategies of yoga that produce a quieting impact. As indicated by specialists, these drills may help lessen pressure and nervousness.

10. IMPROVES VITALITY AND ENERGY: Regular practice of Karate gives strength to your cardiovascular system, empowering your body to release much amount of oxygen to your cerebrum and bloodstream, helping you to feel significantly cautious, sharp and all set.

D. MENTAL BENEFITS OF KARATE:

1. IMPROVES MOOD AND MENTAL TOUGHNESS: The endorphins discharged due to your Karate training can be dynamic in your body for keeping your mood lit up too many hours after you leave the dojo.

2. IMPROVES HUMILITY AND MINDFULNESS: There can always be incredible learning opportunities for Karate students. There is no place for the ego. To be honest, Karate values our qualities and objective about our constraints, shortcomings, and territories that need improvement.

3. IMPROVES PERSEVERANCE: Karate needs a long process of preparation and training to achieve higher belts. Flawlessness comes with hard training. It is just through a determination that you will genuinely prevail in your practice. No martial art starts with immaculate forms and perfect skill; it is the constancy of spirit and assurance to push forward that makes Karateka incredible.

4. IMPROVES RESPECT AND DISCIPLINE: Regard is one of the fundamental principles of Japanese and Chinese hand to hand fighting, and Karate accentuates the significance of regard in all parts of Karate preparation. Students must regard the Sensei as well as other students during their training hours.

5. STRENGTHENS CONCENTRATION AND FOCUS: Working on kicking or punching drills, avoiding an attack, or getting away from a gag requires a lot of mental concentration and focus, bringing about a more elevated level of watchfulness, more grounded subjective control. It may be essential to take note that the act of structures or

Kata requires a great deal of regard for retaining its methods and movements. It will assist you in creating incredible focus abilities.

6. STRENGTHENS EMOTIONAL STATUS: For individuals battling with psychological wellness issues, for example, unhappiness or tension, Karate training can help increase in positiveness. People who practice Karate a few times each week are less vulnerable to pressure and less inclined to be discouraged. Eventually, Karate prompts a more joyful you.

7. INCREASES SELF ESTEEM: When you get familiar with a Karate technique and apply it with your counterpart, you will feel an incredible achievement. This feeling of accomplishment will enable you with confidence and certainty. Karate won't just get you genuinely fit; it will make you feel extraordinary about yourself.

8. ENHANCES CONFIDENCE: The certainty of realizing how to protect yourself and your family is hugely empowering. This certainty will make you a more robust and better individual. It will saturate into our day by day lives, regardless of whether it is at the workplace or in the public place. Self-assurance is a fantastic partner of Karateka.

9. IMPROVES PATIENCE: Rehearsing Karate fighting can show students how to be increasingly persistent. That's why they have the capabilities to counter their opponents at the dojo and outside the dojo.

10. INCREASES INNER CALMNESS AND PEACE: In Karate, during training with an accomplice, you will figure out how to focus on your body movements. It is a ground-breaking type of dynamic contemplation that prompts you to be on top of yourself and your general surroundings. Karate gives you an extraordinary feeling of harmony.

E. CONCLUSION:

In conclusion, the combative technique is a demonstration of self-defense that everybody can adapt effectively. Everybody ought to learn and require combative techniques as it will benefit them in a vast number of ways, particularly these days when safety is never guaranteed. Everybody should learn martial art as it is valuable towards the security of all citizens. Crime percentage and criminals are growing day by day. As the crime percentages are expanding, the correct strategies of self-protection are necessary. Prevention is always better than cure. Life is a blessing. Self-protection assists with setting you up for extraordinary circumstances and creates expanded mental and physical well-being. It might be challenging to envision being attacked by a stranger, yet it happens each day. These attacks occur all of a sudden, and when people do not expect them. By learning the basics of self-protection, you can help yourself in perilous and unanticipated conditions.

*** BASIS OF SHOTOKAN KARATE ***

Shotokan Karate has three sections: Kihon (fundamentals, Kata (examples of moves, and Kumite (fighting. Kihon and Kata are characterized by profound, long positions that give solidness, empower ground-breaking movements, and fortify the legs. At first, quality and power are shown with streaming movements rather than speed. The individuals who progress to dark-coloured and Black Belt levels build up a substantially more advanced style that consolidates hooking, tossing, and some standing joint locking Jiu-Jitsu-like strategies, which can be found even in the fundamental Kata.

1. Kihon (Basics): In Karate, fundamentals are punches, kicks, obstructs, strikes, and positions. Concerning the strong foundation for the karate, we must practice the basics constantly. Basic technique is very important training and must be taken seriously in order to achieve a high level of skills in Karate. Kihon implies Basics. So, to construct a solid establishment for our Karate practitioners, we should rehearse the basics continually. Kihon's training is fundamental to all students and incorporates the act of right body posture and breathing while also rehearsing the fundamentals of thrusts, punches, kicks, and blocks. Kihon's sharpening is significant for Kata's practice, and attention must be required to advance a considerable level of aptitude and spirit.

2. Kata (Forms): Kata is a series of some standardized movements that Karateka use in order to rehearse "offensive" and "defensive" methods without a partner or we can say it is a choreographed sequence of movements or forms. The standards received when learning the basics, including blocks, punches, kicks, and building up an appropriate focal point of gravity, are applied to Kata. Here, the critical point is to utilize these basic moves in an arranged manner. During karate exercises, students figure out how to perform steps in various ways and change positions (starting with one place onto the next). These are the proper movements of Karate and are its pith. There are groups of actions that guard against various imaginary adversaries. Kata contains all the fundamental procedures and positions which are essential to achieve spirit and coordination. Each Kata starts with a Block (Form) to underline the utilization of Karate carefully for self-protection.

3. Kumite (Sparring): Kumite is a stance used to apply hostile and guarded methods rehearsed in the Kata under a progressively reasonable condition where one competitor involves hostile movements and the other, protective strategies. Kata expects non-existent adversaries, while Kumite is repeated with another karateka as a protector or an attacker. Kumite permits the practical use of the moves found in the Kata. It is a type of training that is similar to the act of pre-arranged fighting. Kumite implies partner work or sparring. Basics of Kumite are punches, kicks, blocks, and strikes. Through these drills, we can adequately counter real attacks.

*** PARAMETERS OF SHOTOKAN KATA ***

Kata is a set of Karate moves sorted out into a pre-organized battle against non-existent rivals. The Kata comprises of kicks, punches, strikes, and blocks. Body movements in different Kata incorporate venturing, contorting, turning, dropping, and hopping. In Shotokan Karate, Kata is a presentation or an exhibition that gives specific consideration to speed and timing. Kata is a Japanese word, which means individual training on Karate exercises. Kata is a term that is known widely in the Martial arts world. Kata or schedules of battling can't be just an underlying physical exercise. It is an approach to achieve discipline in Martial art and to develop the art part of it. Without Kata, there is no advancement in Karate-do.

Initially, Gichin Funakoshi chose 15 Kata, which he held as vital to the preparation for Shotokan. These Kata contained its own commonplace conventions of the **Shorin** and **Shorei schools.** These Kata involved fundamental Katas like Heian Shodan, Heian Nidan, Heian Sandan, Heian Yondan, and Heian Godan. These essential Kata originated from the Shorin school, whose Masters showed the standard of fast and incredible movements. Initially, they were designated as "Pinan" Kata until Funakoshi renamed them as "Heian," which signifies "harmony" and "quiet." For him, the three Tekki-Kata likewise had a place with the focal Kata, for example, Bassai-Dai, Kanku-Dai, Empi, Gankaku, Jitte, Hangetsu, and Jion. A few further Kata came later on, for instance, Gojushiho-Kata and Sochin. Today there are 26 Kata in Shotokan Karate.

There are some parameters of Shotokan that must be implemented during performing Katas:

1. Start and end with a **BOW.**

2. Katas are not only the fundamental strategies; there must be steady ease of the actions, like the blood coursing through the veins.

3. There should be no change in movements to assist you.

4. There ought not to be any distortion of moves to make it more distinctive.

5. Fundamental components consist of movements of the body and changes in the speed of the strategies.

6. Breathing must synchronize with corresponding movements of the methods; combined techniques must finish in one breath.

7. Verify that there are precise quantities of actions.

8. Have a watchful posture and sharp upheaval of vocal vitality (**KIAI**).

9. Changing of direction must be done with the help of both hip revolution and supporting leg, with smooth feet movements.

10. The characteristics and importance of every movement are required to demonstrate well.

11. There ought to be appropriate sequencing of procedures.

12. Avoid superfluous movements when moving to start with one strategy onto the next.

13. There must be numerous reiterations of movements to have the option to show the best and proper use of the actions.

14. One check is equivalent to one movement; know about the continuation of counting.

15. All essential strategies ought to be exact.

Kihon's training and authority are fundamental to all propelled preparations and incorporate the act of right body posture and breathing while also rehearsing basics, for example, positions, punches, kicks, obstructions, and pushes. Yet it likewise incorporates basic Kata. Kihon isn't just repeating strategies; similarly, Budoka encourages the right soul and demeanour consistently. Kihon strategies should be refined regularly, as a rule during each training session. They are viewed as essential to authority and improvement of all movements of more remarkable intricacy.

*** DEMEANOUR AND ATTITUDE DURING A COMPETITION ***

A. FOR KATA:

1. On the declaration of your name, respond with a noisy "**OSS**."

2. Walk carefully to the edge of the ring, straightforwardly at your start position.

3. "**BOW**" perfectly.

4. Having finished your Kata, hold up in the "**YOI**" position for your scores to be declared or a demonstration of banners to show the champion.

5. Walk and turn around, without looking behind, bow at the edge of the competition area, and leave.

B. FOR KUMITE:

1. On the declaration of your name, respond with an energetic "**OSS**" and walk astutely to the edge of the competition area, at your start position.

2. At the referee's order, bow at the edge of the challenging territory and walk gladly to your beginning position.

3. On "**HAJIME**," move forward, finishing off with Kamae with an energetic "**KIAI**."

4. Never bow on "**HAJIME**."

5. On "**YAME**," stop quickly and move back to your start position, never turn your back towards your rival.

6. Refrain from demonstrating your pain to opponents during the competition.

7. If your opponent gets harmed, don't stoop down with your back to your competitor; hold the "**YOI**" position confronting your adversary.

8. Upon scoring a point, don't turn your back or celebrate in triumph over your adversary; keep battling until "**YAME**" is heard.

9. Never question a judge's decision. Surrender every one of the inquiries over to your supervisor.

10. Never address your opponent while going up against him. Towards the end of the match, "**BOW**" to your competitor.

*** SIGNIFICANT NOTES TO REMEMBER WHEN GRADING ***

A. FOR ORGANIZATION:

1. Ensure that all charges, for example, association charges, education costs, and evaluating expenses, are paid in advance.

2. Verify that the member's name, date of birth, and the present year's enlistment have been accurately entered in the member Shotokan Karate enrollment book with the rubber stamp on it.

3. Always reach with much time to save before the evaluating assessment, to guarantee the reviewing structure has been finished and evaluating expenses paid.

4. After a fruitful KYU evaluation, a declaration must be introduced to the member at no additional charge.

5. The Shotokan Karate KYU reviewing elastic stamp must be put in the member's Shotokan Karate participation book, and the evaluation must be recorded upon the arrival of the review by the approved reviewing official.

B. FOR DRESS:

1. An unironed clean white Karate-do Gi, with a Shotokan Karate identification sewn on the left-hand side of the Karate do-Gi coat.

2. The first name to be imprinted on the left half of the Karate do-Gi (printed down along the crease).

3. Belt should be properly tied.

4. Karateka must not wear slipper or personal shoes.

5. Ensure that no Karateka should wear ring, chain, or bracelet.

C. FOR DISPOSITION:

1. Correct disposal must be held consistently during the reviewing process.

2. When called by a senior (particularly the evaluating board), respond with an energetic **OSS**, followed by a snappy obliging **BOW**. Guidelines ought to be executed as fast as could be expected under the circumstances.

3. While reviewing, verify that assessment is performed with 100% correctness.

4. Remember that the method for Karate ignores race, religion, or social standing.

5. Students should both attack and guard with as much energy as possible during an evaluation process.

*** SHOTOKAN KARATE PICTORIAL STANCES WITH DESCRIPTION ***

When using attacking and defensive techniques, the body has to be in a state of balance or equilibrium in order to be effective. Good form, proper stance is the foundation of strong and efficient techniques. The upper body must be kept straight, the hips parallel to the floor, and balance must be kept to be able to use maximum speed and power. Strong and effective techniques come from a strong stance. Stances were historically created from diligent research of Pioneer Masters and resulted in being the foundation of modern KARATE-DO. There are two types of positions. One has the influential position of pushing the knees outward and the other, inward. Concerning first, both knees progressively "push" outwards while the inner thighs remain strained. The Kata incorporates all the Karate stances. Control and mind balance are some watchwords that characterizes a best Karateka. Winning a fight is not is not the main concern in the Karate, but it is te best proficient method of utilizing the human body to learn self-defense through blocking, punching, and kicking procedures. It adjusts both the body and brain too. Irrespective of the fact that this game shows the art of self-defense and attack to the Karateka, the one and only the objective is the personal growth. Thus, at this crossroads, here is a brief outline of delineating the Karate **with high-resolution photos** for you to understand easily. So, let's go to explore the world of Shotokan Karate stances.

1. YOKO GERI: The side edge of the foot is to execute a sideways attack on the opponent's solar plexus, the groin, or the facial area from the sides or front. There are two sorts of sidekicks: the side snaps kick and the side push kick.

2. NIDAN GERI: It is a double jump kick and the last move in Kata Kanku-Dai. This kick can be practiced by both the legs. Firstly, I took fighting stance with right leg on the backside and then took a jump by extending right leg to the upward side to make a double jump kick. I have performed it through step-wise jumping (four steps in one photo) so that all Karateka can easily understand it.

3. YOKO TOBI GERI: I have executed it in phases (four steps in one photo), in the picture. The flying side kick comes in force for an unexpected attack; however, it has the role of retaliation to the chest or neck.

4. UCHI UKE: It is known as the inside lower arm obstruction. This essential blockade is utilized to redirect attacks to the midriff. It starts with the blocking hand under the opposite armpit with the palm down. The arm is pulled outward while turning the wrist. Toward the completion, the arm is bent at a 90-degree angle.

5. SHUTO UKE: Blade hand obstruction. The blade hand block uses the blade edge of the hand to hinder the attack directed at the midriff, chest or face. On finishing, the shutting hand is held out with the palm facing forward and the side edge striking the assailant's wrist while the other hand is kept before the solar plexus.

6. SOTO UKE: This block has the arm moving from the outside to inside. As a block, it can secure against a forward strike to confront, a forward strike to the chest, a forward strike to stomach region, neck, and a roundhouse to head.

7. YOKO GERI KEKOMI: Side straight kick. This method is like the side snap kick, except that it has a more drawn out range. For this kick, the knee is raised to the front of the body, with the foot beside another knee. Chamber the leg by pushing the side edge of the foot towards the target.

SHOTOKAN KARATE: EASIEST WAY TO GET BLACK BELT

8. YOKO GERI KEAGE: It is a standing upwards side-kick. This kick is used against an attacker in close range. It is performed by using the edge of the foot as the striking technique. Bring the knee up to the side, with the kicking foot against the other knee and toes curled up. The side edge of the foot is snapped outward.

9. HIZA GERI: This technique is viable mainly when an aggressor obstructs a front kick. It might be performed straight upward to the front or in a circular segment from the side to the front. It is applied against an assailant's belly, solar plexus, chest, ribs or face.

10. GYAKU ZUKI: This turn around attack is used to maintain a strategic distance from an adversary or response after an obstruction. Execution is from a Front Stance, turning the hips totally and driving the arm forward.

11. URAKEN UCHI: This procedure utilizes the snapping movement of the elbow to hit the target with the help of the back of clenched hands. It is used fundamentally as an attack on the face, solar plexus or sides of the body.

SHOTOKAN KARATE: EASIEST WAY TO GET BLACK BELT

12. MOROTE YOKO ZUKI: It is a double fist side punch.

13. MOROTE ZUKI JODAN: Double "U" shaped punch at face level.

14. KIZAMI ZUKI: The hit punch is executed by compellingly fixing the arm while utilizing the intensity of the hips and back leg to attack. The punch is quick and conclusive.

15. GEDAN BARAI: The descending obstruction is utilized to redirect a strike or kick to the outside of the body that is aimed at the belly or crotch. It is performed with the lower arm as a blocking device while turning the wrist.

16. SUKUI UKE: Scooping obstruction. The scooping blockade strategy comprises of scooping the aggressor's leg with the lower arm and breaking their equilibrium. Bring the lower arm underneath the assailant's leg and scoop it away from the body.

17. RENOJI DACHI: In the L-position, the feet position is in the state of the letter 'L.' Legs are one shoulder-width separated from heel to heel. Knees are marginally bent, and the front foot is pointing ahead.

18. JIYU IPPON KUMITE: To stop the attack and respond to the attack. Free-form one-advance competing is like one-advance fighting. However, it requires the Karateka to be moving. Rehearsing one-advance competing enhances free fighting (Jiyu Kumite) aptitudes, and gives a chance to repeating significant counter-attack (instead of minor counter-attack). Tsutomu Ohshima states that free-form one-advance fighting is the most sensible practice in Shotokan Karate and that it is more reasonable than free competing.

19. YAMA ZUKI: Like the U punch, the mountain punch utilizes both, fore-clenched or fore-fisted hands to attack the head and the abdomen. The upper arm goes from over the head in a marginally bent way to the face while the lower arm pursues a straight approach to the stomach.

20. YOI DACHI: Ready position. The YOI position is a preliminary position that gives the beginning stage for the execution of different styles. In other words, the principle adaptation of YOI implies that the arms are marginally pushed ahead, with clenched hands. The elbows ought to be bent slightly.

21. OSAE UKE: Palm press. Like the broad obstruct, this method is utilized against a low attack just to the mid-region or crotch. The assailant's arm is pushed down, and the retaliation is implemented at the same time.

22. KOKUTSU DACHI: Back Stance. The front leg slightly bent, and 70% of the weight stays on the back leg. Both legs are in "L" shape. The back leg is curved precisely like Straddling Horse Stance (KIBA-DACHI), and the front leg is widened. On the other hand, the feet make the 90-degree angle. The chest region is kept straight and sideways.

SHOTOKAN KARATE: EASIEST WAY TO GET BLACK BELT

23. SHIKO DACHI: This block position is like the straddle-leg position, and the left foot is turned 45-degrees in the left, and right foot is 45-degrees on the right side. Knees should be bent, and the chest should be straight. This stance is for protection from side attacks.

24. JODAN MAE GERI: Raising the leg towards the sky covers the upper level, i.e., face, neck, and head area of the opponent. The front kick comprises raising the knee and kicking outward from the body. The striking surface is the pad of the foot. There are two sorts of front kicks: the front snap kick and the front push kick.

SHOTOKAN KARATE: EASIEST WAY TO GET BLACK BELT

25. TATE URAKEN UCHI: It's a vertical back fist attack.

26. UCHI OTOSHI UKE: The dropping block is utilized to divert a punch. It comprises of dropping the arm to wreck the assailant's lower arm.

27. NEKO ASHI DACHI: Cat Stance. It has full movement of your front leg, so this can be twisted to deflect kicks to your legs and groin area. The front foot is pointed forward and on just the ball of foot. The back foot is oriented around 45 degrees with the leg strained. 80 % of body weight is on back leg and 20 % of weight is on the front leg.

28. AGE UKE: Rising obstruction. The rising blockade, also called an upward block, is utilized to avoid attacks over the solar plexus. It is fundamentally executed with a fist even though it might be framed with many hand positions. Block upward with the outer side of the lower arm.

SHOTOKAN KARATE: EASIEST WAY TO GET BLACK BELT

29. MAWASHI GERI: The roundhouse kick can be implemented from the front or back leg against an objective in front or marginally to the side. The leg swings sideways in a circular segment from outside utilizing the snap of the knee.

30. KOSA DACHI: The X-position is frequently utilized when coming down from a bounce or turning. It comprises putting one foot behind or before the other and bearing all weight on one foot.

SHOTOKAN KARATE: EASIEST WAY TO GET BLACK BELT

31. JUJI UKE: There are two sorts of X-blocks: (1) blocking upward to avoid an attack to the face, and (2) blocking by descending to divert a kick to the stomach or crotch. The block is typically performed from the forward or corner-to-corner straddle-leg position.

32. USHIRO GERI: In the back kick, the heel is utilized as the striking surface in attacking the back. There are two sorts of back kicks: the back-snap kick and the back-push kick.

33. CHUDAN UCHI UKE: This essential block is utilized to redirect attacks to the midriff. It starts with the blocking hand under the opposite armpit with the palm down, and the arm is pulled outward.

34. EMPI UCHI: Elbow attack. A variety of elbow strikes. This method is utilized to strike appropriately on the back with the elbow. It uses a similar movement as pulling back the hand to the side when punching. Targets are the assailant's chest or waist.

35. MAE GERI: A front kick is performed by lifting the knee of the kicking leg to abdomen stature and, afterwards, pushing the all-inclusive leg forward to hit the objective with the pad of the foot.

36. FUMIKOMI GERI: While performing the front, and back-stepping kick, the heel is utilized as the striking surface. Targets are the knee joint, shin, lower leg and instep.

SHOTOKAN KARATE: EASIEST WAY TO GET BLACK BELT

37. HEISOKU DACHI: A position that stands straight, with shoulders and legs relaxed or loose, hands to the side. Feet are joined together, and the weight is equally appropriated on each foot.

[81]

38. MOROTE UKE: Move the fist of extending arm close to the elbow of the blocking arm and block firmly at action time.

39. KAKIWAKE UKE: This stance is a twofold block wherein the external wrists are utilized to obstruct a double clenched hand punch or to safeguard against an aggressor who tries to grab you by the neck.

40. HAISHU UKE: The backhand block is utilized to counter a punch to the chest or solar plexus by hitting the assailant's upper arm, lower arm, or elbow. Block with the backhand, keeping the hand and wrist straight and utilizing a springing movement of the elbow.

41. ZENKUTSU DACHI: Front Stance. A position with the bent front leg. It is an entirely steady position with the 70% weight of the body resting on the front leg.

42. SANCHIN DACHI: It may be portrayed very well as Uchi Hachiji Dachi with one foot pushed ahead until the toes of the back foot are on a similar level line as the impact point of the front foot.

SHOTOKAN KARATE: EASIEST WAY TO GET BLACK BELT

43. SAGI ASHI DACHI: In the heron leg position, the underside of the lifted foot is put against within the knee of the standing leg.

44. TSURU ASHI DACHI: The crane position is utilized to keep away from attacks and to progress into different methods. One leg is raised, and its instep is placed behind the knee of the standing leg.

45. YOKO EMPI: This side elbow strike is like Empi in which the elbow is pushed decidedly sideways to land at the target. The lower arm should be relentlessly flexed inwards to strike forward, backward, and sideways.

46. URA ZUKI: The shut punch focuses on the face, waist, or side of the body and is applied with the palm turned inward or upward, punching straight ahead with the fore-clenched hand. It is powerful for short proximity battling. Keep the elbow near the body and chest muscles tense.

47. SEIKEN ZUKI: Proper fist attack. Seiken Zuki is to punch with the clenched hand so that the joint of the center finger (2 knuckles) will hit the rival.

48. SOKUME: It is a side combined block.

SHOTOKAN KARATE: EASIEST WAY TO GET BLACK BELT

49. MAE KEAGE GERI: A snapped movement by a front kick. The most widely recognized kick in karate. For this kick, the pad of foot is customarily utilized; however, the instep or pointed toes may also be used. To play out a front snap kick, turn the kicking leg pointedly, lifting the knee high and near the chest.

50. UCHI UKE GEDAN BARAI: It is a Block from inside to outside at the lower level or near knee of leg area.

51. TATE EMPI UCHI: It is a vertical elbow attack.

52. TETTSUI UCHI: It's also called fist attack like hammer.

53. TEISHO AWASE UKE: It is known as a combined hands block.

SHOTOKAN KARATE: EASIEST WAY TO GET BLACK BELT

54. TATE SHUTO UKE: It is known as upright knife-hand obstruction.

55. KATA HIZA DACHI: It's a one knee stance.

56. OI ZUKI: To play out a rush punch, move into a forward position by sliding one foot forward, punching simultaneously with the fore-clenched hand on the propelling foot of the attacker.

57. IAIGOSHI DACHI: This kneeling position is regularly used to strike an adversary who is laying down. It is framed by stooping on one knee with the toes of that foot on the floor. The other foot is about a clench hand width before and to the side of the knee on the floor. The upstanding knee is straightforwardly over the toes of the front foot. This position comprises of bowing on the back leg.

58. TEISHO UCHI: The palm-heel strike can be performed upward or from the side and uses the impact point of the palm as the striking surface. It is utilized to attack the face, jaw, ribs, solar plexus, and to block an attack. To play out the upward palm-heel strike, push the striking hand upward and outward from the midriff.

59. MOROTE URA ZUKI: It is a double handed close punch.

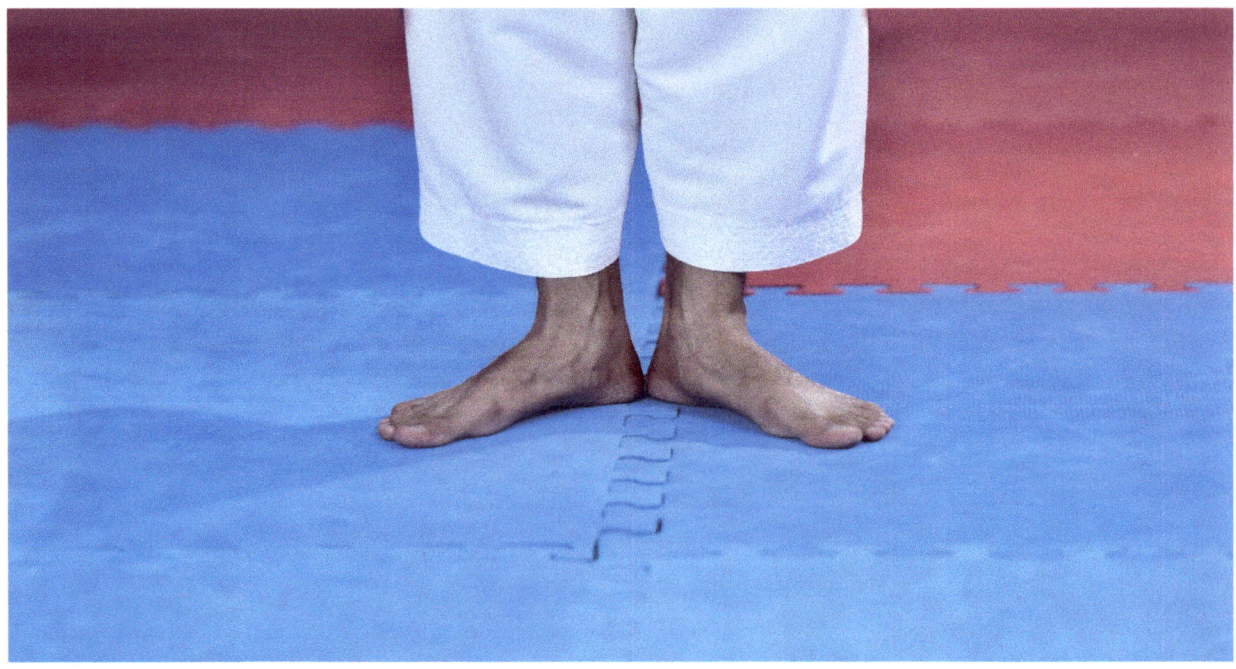

60. MUSUBI DACHI: In the consideration position, heels are joined together as one, yet the toes open at a 45-degree angle. This position is utilized to play out a conventional bow.

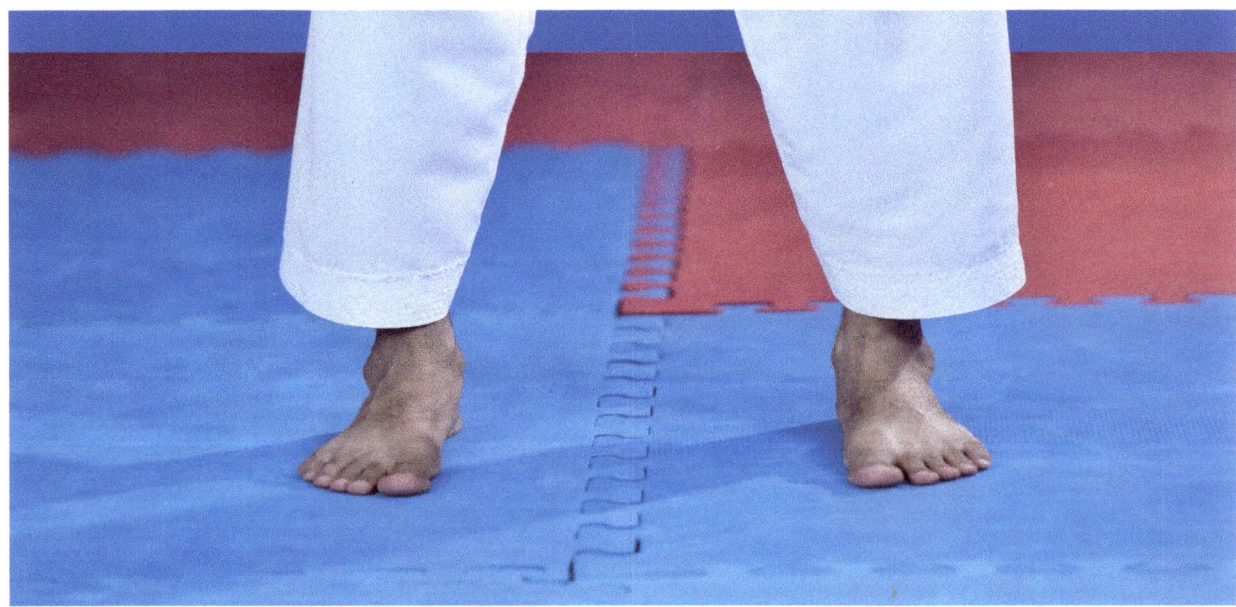

61. HEIKO DACHI: Feet parallel to shoulder with natural stance. The feet are one shoulder-width separated, pointing ahead. Hands are in a clenched position along the edges.

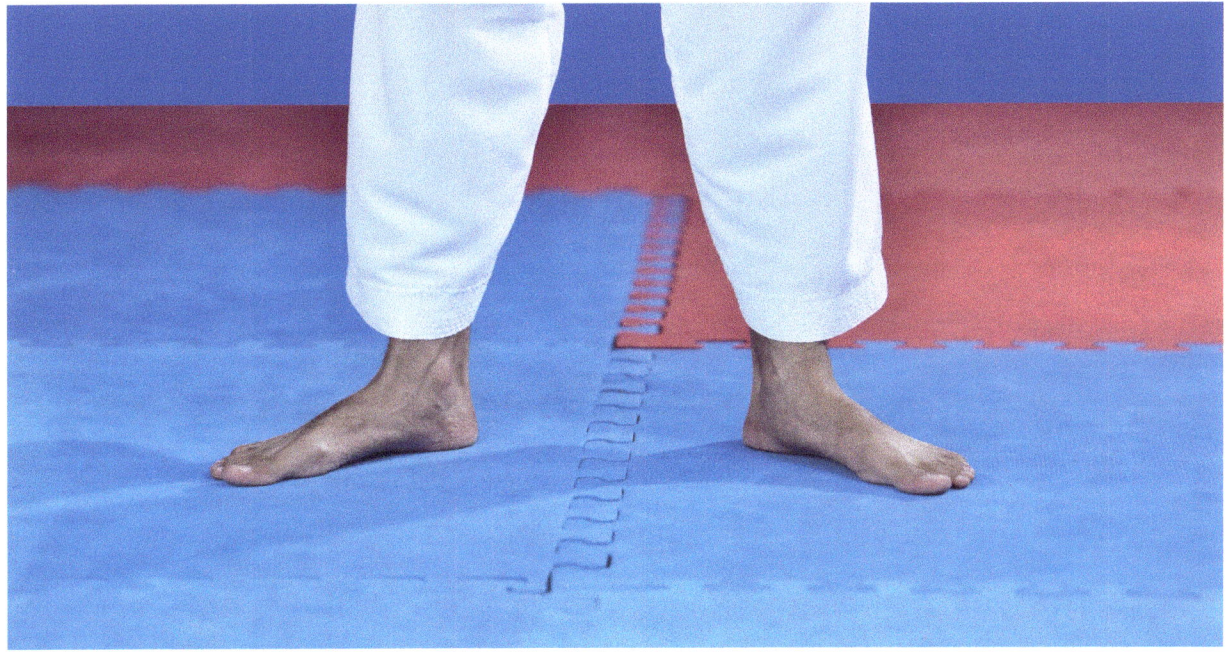

62. HACHIJI DACHI: A specific position where Legs are one shoulder-width separated with toes marginally outward at a 45-degree angle. Legs are straight, hands are straight, slightly apart from the body, and the body is relaxed.

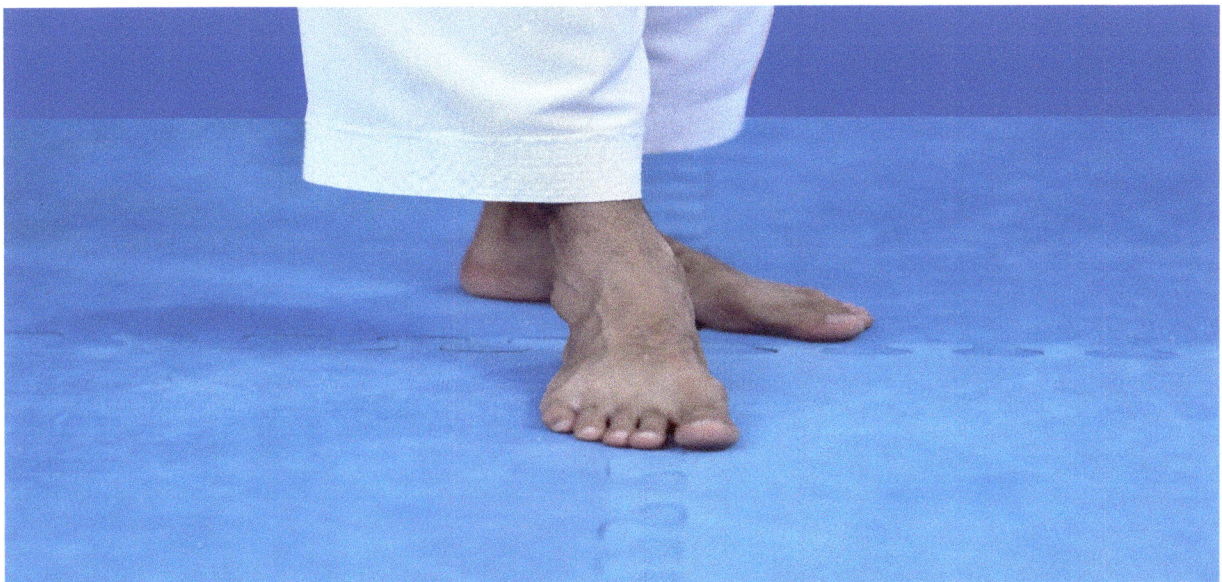

63. TEIJI DACHI: Feet are one shoulder-width apart, and the front foot is pointing ahead, concentrating on keeping along the middle of the back leg. In the T-position, the feet form a 'T' shape. Legs are slightly bent.

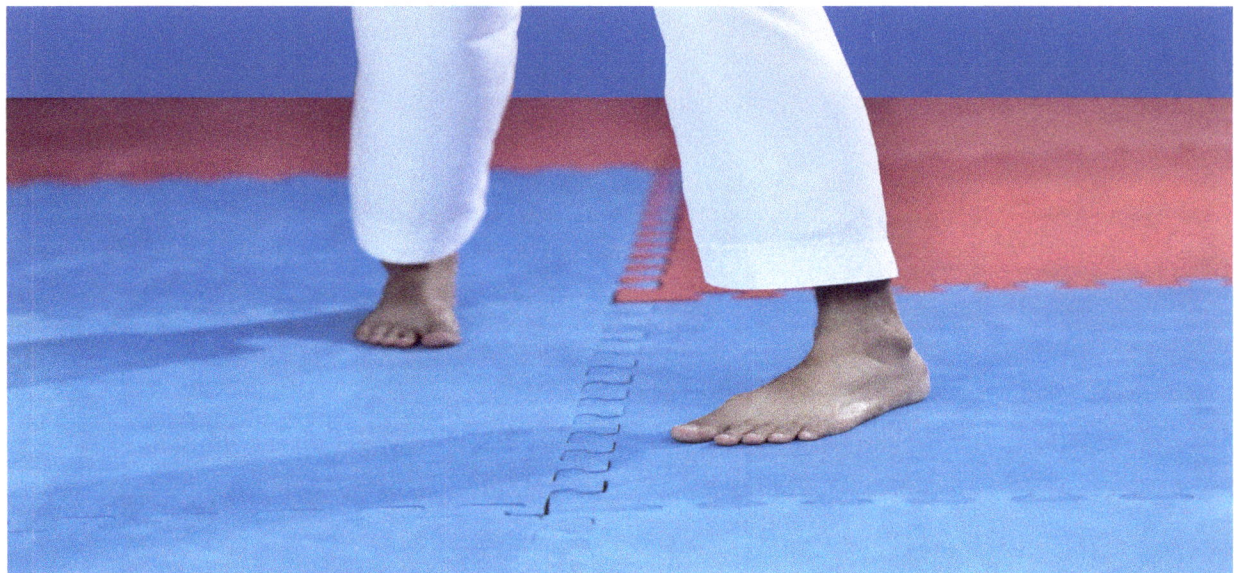

64. HANGETSU DACHI: For this Half-moon position, the feet are around two shoulder widths separated, and the weight is equally conveyed on the two feet. The feet are turned inward, and the body is in the forward-looking position. To push ahead or in reverse, the foot goes roundly.

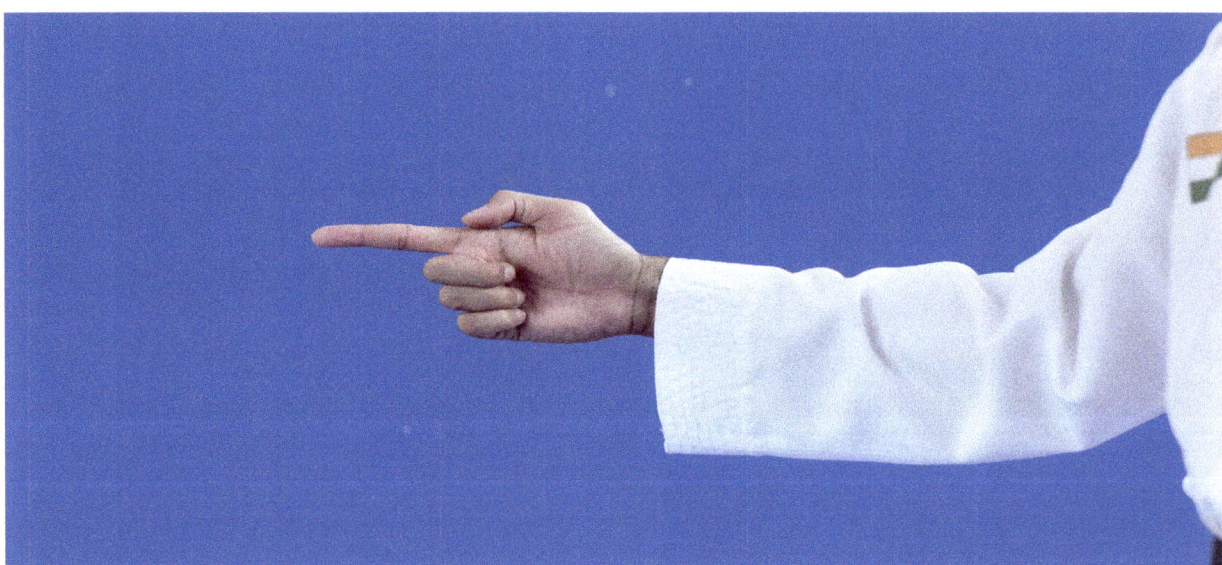

65. IPPON KUMITE: The index finger is stretched out forward while other fingers are twisted into the palm, and the thumb bends firmly against the side of the center finger. It is utilized to attack the eye, beneath the nose, the throat, or the lower rib region. For best outcomes, index finger ought to be twisted marginally inwards.

66. NUKITE UCHI: It is also known as a fingers attack.

67. KIBA DACHI: Horse-riding stance. Weight centered on both the bent legs. It's like a soldier sitting on a horse and fighting with an enemy. Feet are parallel and wide with the back straight.

68. SHUTO UCHI: A Knife hand attack. The blade hand strike can be conveyed either from inside to outside or from outside to inside. Targets are the sanctuary, carotid corridor, and side of the body. The striking hand comes high to the side of the head to play out the outside blade hand strike.

69. SOCHIN DACHI: The established position is a mix of the forward position and the straddle-leg position. The body is low, and the legs are spread, around two shoulder widths apart. The knees are bent, and both feet are at a 45-degree angle inside the line of movement. The weight is evenly distributed on both the feet. It's like Fudo Dachi stance.

70. MIKAZUKI GERI: The sickle kick is utilized as either an attack or a blockade, and it uses the level bottom of the foot as the striking surface to attack the solar plexus, ribs or face. Its line of movement to the objective looks like the state of a half-moon.

71. JODAN JUJI UKE: Upper-level blockings. There are two kinds of cross blocks: (1) blocking upward to redirect an attack to the face, and (2) blocking downward to divert a kick to the belly or crotch. The blocks are customarily performed from the forward or corner to corner straddle-leg position.

72. REI OR BOW: An expression of regard and honor given to the opponent or Sensei, in the beginning or end of the match.

MISCELLANEOUS PHOTOS ON SHOTOKAN KARATE

The author at the premises of the Shotokan Karate Academy, India.

The author performing side leg splitting exercise at the Shotokan Karate Academy, India.

The author executing One Arm Hand Stand exercise at the Shotokan Karate Academy, India.

The author with the legendary World Karate Federation's 3rd DAN Certificate.

The author with daughter Tanaya at the Shotokan Karate academy, India.

*** HONORARY RANKING IN SHOTOKAN KARATE ***

Master Jigoro Kano, a Japanese man who is supposed to be the originator of present Judo, was the first to concoct the colored belt framework. He imagined that it would be a successful point to see the Karateka progress and granted the first "Black belts" around 1880. At that point, Master Gichin Funakoshi, embraced the belt positioning art utilized in ranking system to facilitate mentor to evaluate the grade of their progress at different levels which encourages the progress of martial arts efficaciously. I have just enlightened you about the most considerable degree Black Belt and what it fundamentally implies, i.e., the dominance of the essential strategies alongside mental advancement, which is necessary to make them successful.

1. SHODAN—FIRST DAN. This rank is imperative to the sensei. At the point when somebody has accomplished Shodan, they have demonstrated a devotion to the sensei's lessons and standards and have shown themselves to be commendable for the sensei's endeavours.

2. NIDAN—SECOND DAN. This rank is the level at which the Karateka has aced the fundamentals. It implies that the Karateka is presently ready to play out the methods all the more precipitously, and with more speed, power, and effortlessness.

3. SANDAN—THIRD DAN. The students have to figure out how to turn the whole body to gain speed. Empi (elbow) methods are additionally first time learned in this Kata.

4. YONDAN—FOURTH DAN. This rank is commonly viewed as the primary showing level of Karate. That is, an individual who achieves Yondan ought to have the option to freely deliver Shodan, taking the students from White Belt to Black Belt with no outside assistance.

5. GODAN—FIFTH DAN. This rank holder is having aced with the extra ordinary skills about Karate. Individuals accomplishing Godan have most likely been rehearsing relentlessly for, in any event, 25 years and have an incredibly profound comprehension of their technique and because of their preparation, of themselves.

6. ROKUDAN—SIXTH DAN. This rank utilizes a Kiba Dachi position. Rokudan uses low blocks and centre punch. Rokudan is also called a Kihon Kata.

7. SHICHIDAN—SEVENTH DAN. This level shows that the individual achieving it has done extensive testing of his Rokudan and has applied it generally in the precise application.

8. HACHIDAN—EIGHTH DAN. One who is familiar with the puzzles of Karate procedure, hypothesis, or educating and have altogether developed in their aptitudes.

9. KUDAN—NINTH DAN. This level is typically saved for those few people who have devoted their whole lives to Karate-do remarkably. An individual achieving Kudan is believed to be the living exemplification of the absolute best characteristics a person can create through a commitment to Karate-do.

10. JUDAN—TENTH DAN. This grade is typically saved for the Master of a style, even though it is, at times, granted to individuals who have accomplished a degree of regard distinctly to the heads of styles. In numerous associations, Judan is given plainly to pay tribute to the passing of the head of a reputed Karate style. There are not many genuine Judan in Karate-do, neither past nor present. A few associations don't grant higher than the fifth DAN.

*** SHOTOKAN KARATE PERIOD FOR DAN GRADES ***

Some broad rules were framed in the late 1960s by the Federation of All-Japan Karate-do Organizations, and these rules still, by and large, mirror the base time in level benchmarks utilized by most Japanese Karate associations:

1. **1st DAN:** It requires more than two years of independent practice.
2. **2nd DAN:** It requires more than two years after first DAN.
3. **3rd DAN:** It requires more than three years after the second DAN.
4. **4th DAN:** It requires more than four years after the third DAN.
5. **5th DAN:** It requires more than five years after the fourth DAN.
6. **6th DAN:** It requires more than six years after the fifth DAN.
7. **7th DAN:** It requires more than seven years after the sixth DAN in addition to a base age necessity of 40 years.
8. **8th DAN:** It requires more than eight years after the seventh DAN, in addition to a base age necessity of 50 years.
9. **9th DAN:** It requires more than nine years after the eighth DAN, in addition to a base age necessity of 60 years.
10. **10th DAN:** It requires more than ten years after the ninth DAN, in addition to a base age necessity of 70 years.

Remember that these are absolute minimum time prerequisites. Keep in mind that it was conceivable to accomplish first-degree Black Belt in a short span. However, the vast majority take somewhere in the range of three to five years. It is a similar path with the progressed DAN rankings: they quite often take longer than the base, which records for a great deal of the wearing down. Be that as it may, a higher degree can be accomplished, subject to Karateka's authority and aptitudes for the particular higher evaluations.

For instance, how about we accept that you start Karate preparation at 25 and, being liberal, suppose that you make first DAN at the age of

28 and are now holding a first-degree Black Belt. Suppose, additionally, that you are a genuine wizard at Karate, and you make each propelled positioning in the base measure of time. Along these lines, it takes you more years to make it to second DAN; at 30 years of age. Third DAN comes at the age of 33; fourth DAN comes at 37; fifth DAN makes it to you at 42, and sixth DAN makes it to you at 48. At seventh DAN, you are 55, and at eighth DAN, you are 63. By then, you have nine years to sit tight for ninth DAN, which you would get at 72. Typically, just the Master of a style gets tenth DAN. So, you likely don't need to stress over it. In specific associations, tenth DAN is granted posthumously.

A second-degree Black Belt sensibly takes somewhere in the period of 5 and 8 years of preparation, and a third-degree Black Belt once in a while happens with less than 10 to 12 years. Achieving a fourth-degree Black Belt seldom happens without 15 to 20 years of experience, and it's elusive to be a fifth-degree Black Belt for anybody who hasn't been around in any event for 25 years that makes you 50 years old, with approximately eight years to sit tight for the sixth degree. When we enlighten you about the precise prerequisites for the rankings, you'll see it to be significantly simpler to make sense of why there are so few seventh, eighth, and nine DANs. Nonetheless, a Black Belt can indeed be achieved early, subject to Karetaka's skills, commitment, and mastery in the field.

SHOTOKAN KARATE: EASIEST WAY TO GET BLACK BELT

*** LAYOUT OF KUMITE COMPETITION AREA ***

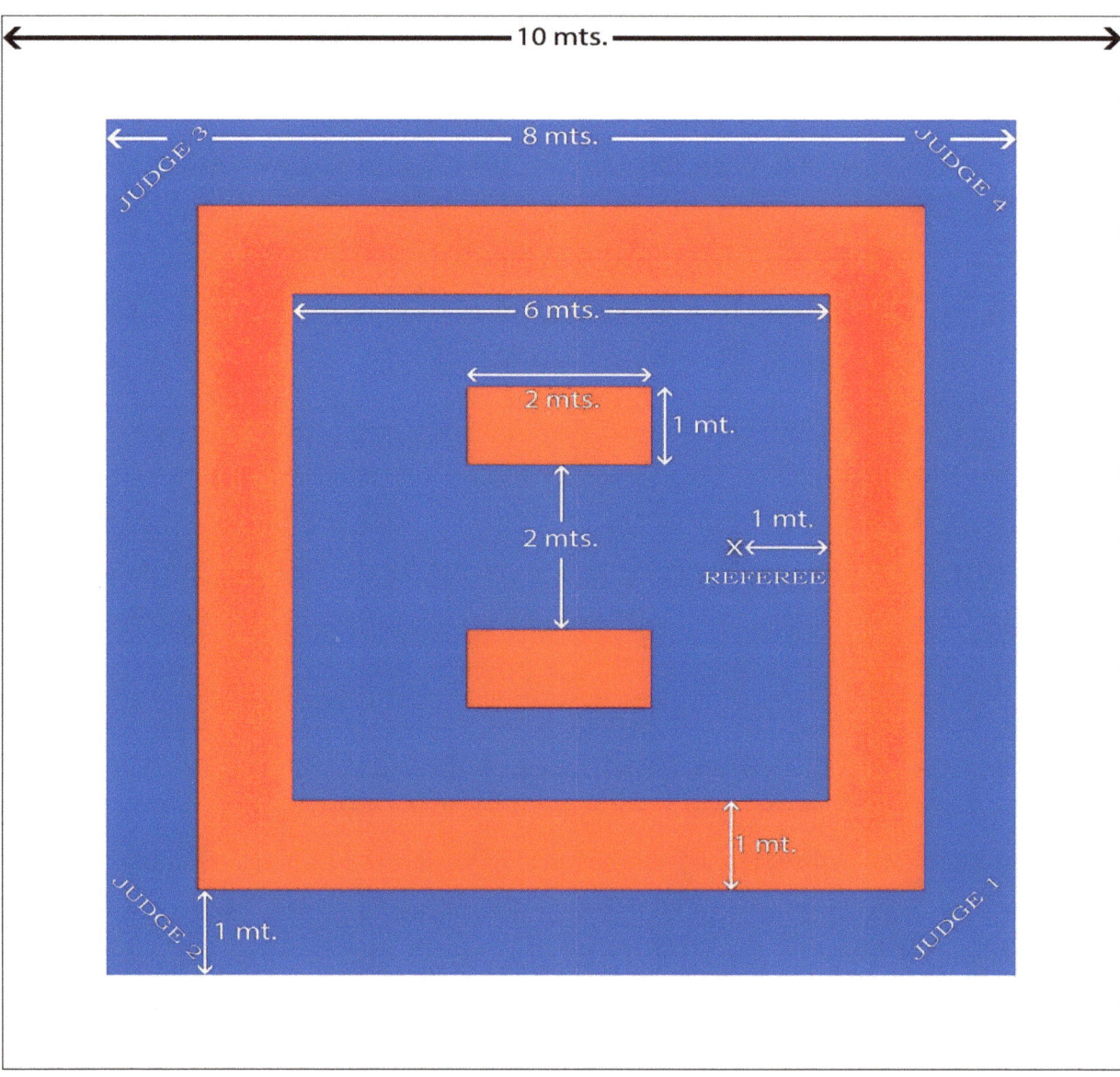

The layout of Kumite competition area will consist of the following points:

1. The competition area of 8 meters from outside will be a WKF authorized matted square, consisting of a one-meter safety area from all sides.

2. A line will be drawn 2 meters from the focal point of the competition area or 1 meter from the inside edge of the red mat of the competition area for the Referee to stand.

3. Each Judge will be seated in the safety area at the corners of the mat.

4. The Match Supervisor will sit at any side of the Referee or behind him outside the safety area.

5. The score chief will sit at the official score table, between the scorekeeper and the timekeeper.

6. Each Judge will be positioned at the corners on the carpet in the safety zone. The Referee may move around the whole tatami, including the secured area where the Judges are positioned. Each Judge will have a red and a blue banner.

SHOTOKAN KARATE: EASIEST WAY TO GET BLACK BELT

*** LAYOUT OF KATA COMPETITION AREA ***

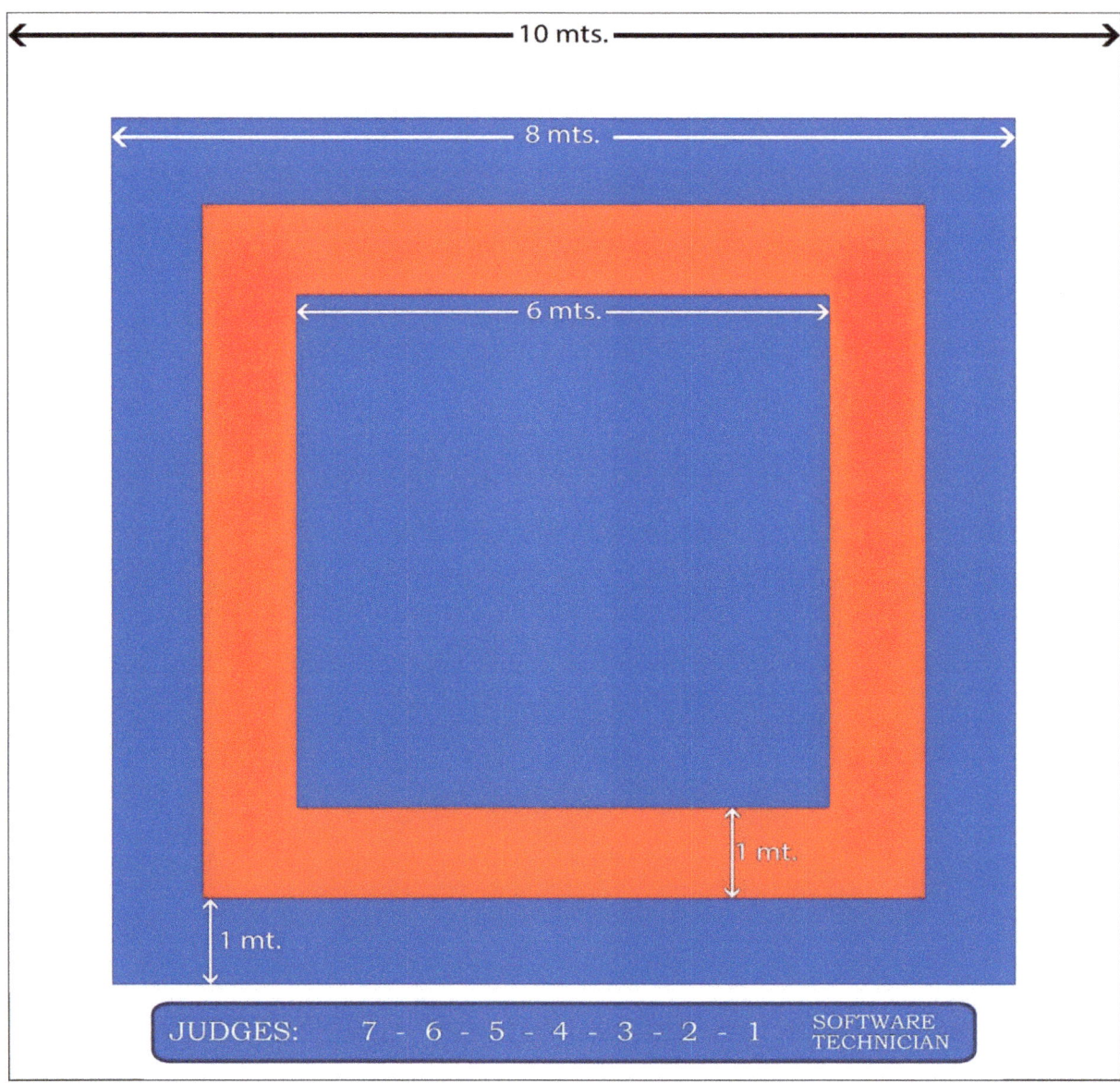

The layout of Kata competition area will consist of the following points:
1. The competition area for Kumite is utilized for Kata as well.

2. The mats are to be of uniform shading, but an external one meter must be of a different colour.

3. Judges will sit next to each other at a table facing the competitors, and judge No. 1 will sit nearest to the Software Technician.

SHOTOKAN KARATE: EASIEST WAY TO GET BLACK BELT

*** SHOTOKAN KARATE KYU EXAMINATIONS ***
*** WHITE BELT TO YELLOW BELT ***
(9th KYU TO 8th KYU)

Note: ↑ Advance moving

↓ Reverse moving

↔ Repeat the method

Coach to check that every procedure is to be exhibited multiple times.

Kihon

From Zenkutsu Dachi – Gedan Barai

1) ↑ Oi Zuki Chudan

2) ↑ Gyaku Zuki Chudan

3) ↑ Age Uke

4) ↑ Soto Uke

5) ↑ Uchi Uke

Change position to Kokutsu Dachi

6) ↑ Shuto Uke

Change position to Zenkutsu Dachi

7) ↑↑ ↔ Mae Geri (hands on the side)

Change position to Kiba Dachi

8) ↑↑ ↔ Yoko Geri Keage (hands on the side)

Kata –

Heian Shodan

Kumite – Coach to check

Gohon Kumite – 5-time attack and block.

Jodan

Chudan

Mae Geri

Start from left-hand side or right-hand side (instructor's decision).

*** YELLOW BELT TO ORANGE BELT ***
(8th KYU TO 7th KYU)

Note: ↑ Advance moving

↓ Reverse moving

↔ Repeat the method

Coach to check – every procedure to be exhibited multiple times.

Kihon

From Zenkutsu Dachi – Gedan Barai

1) ↑ Oi Zuki Chudan

2) ↑ Gyaku Zuki Chudan

3) ↓ Age Uke and Gyaku Zuki

4) ↑ Soto Uke and Gyaku Zuki

5) ↓ Uchi Uke and Gyaku Zuki

Change position to Kokutsu Dachi

6) ↑ Shuto Uke

Change position to Zenkutsu Dachi

7) ↑ Mae Geri (hands on the side)

8) ↑ Mawashi Geri (hands on the side)

Change position to Kiba Dachi

9) ↑↑ ↔ Yoko Geri Keage (hands on the side)

10) ↑↑ ↔ Yoko Geri Kekomi (hands on the side)

Kata – analyst totally

Heian Nidan

Kumite – Coach to check

Sanbon Kumite – 3-time attack and protection

Jodan, Chudan and Mae Geri

Start from left-hand side or right-hand side (instructor's decision).

*** ORANGE BELT TO GREEN BELT ***
(7th KYU TO 6th KYU)

Note: ↑ Advance moving

↓ Reverse moving

↔ Repeat the method

Karate-ka to show every position multiple times.

Kihon

From Zenkutsu Dachi – Gedan Barai

1) ↑ Sanbon Zuki: (Jodan, Chudan and again Chudan)

2) ↑ Sanbon Gyaku Zuki (Chudan, Jodan and Chudan)

3) ↓ Age Uke and Gyaku Zuki

4) ↑ Soto Uke and Gyaku Zuki

5) ↓ Uchi Uke and Gyaku Zuki

6) ↑ Spinning Gyaku Zuki

Change position to Kokutsu Dachi

7) ↑ Shuto Uke

Change position to Zenkutsu Dachi

8) ↑ Mae Geri (hands-on sides)

9) ↑↑ ↔ Mawashi Geri (hands-on sides)

Change position to Kiba Dachi

10) ↑↑ ↔ Yoko Geri Keage (hands on the sides)

11) ↑↑ ↔ Yoko Geri Kekomi (hands on the sides)

Kata

Heian Sandan

Kumite – Examiner to tally.

Kihon Ippon Kumite – 1-time attack and block.

Jodan X 1

Chudan X 1

Mae Geri X 1

SENIORS - Counter with Gyaku Zuki.

Start from left-hand side or right-hand side (instructor's decision).

SHOTOKAN KARATE: EASIEST WAY TO GET BLACK BELT

*** GREEN BELT TO BLUE BELT ***
(6th KYU TO 5th KYU)

Note: ↑ Advance moving

↓ Reverse moving

↔ Repeat the method

Karate-ka to show every strategy multiple times.

Kihon

From Zenkutsu Dachi – Gedan Barai

1) ↑ Sanbon Zuki: (Jodan, Chudan and again Chudan)

2) ↑ Sanbon Gyaku Zuki

3) ↓ Age Uke and Gyaku Zuki

4) ↑ Soto Uke (Empi in Kiba Dachi stance)

5) ↑ Uchi Uke, Kizami Zuki and Gyaku Zuki

6) ↓ Spinning Gyaku Zuki

Change position to Kokutsu Dachi

7) ↑ Shuto Uke (Nukite in Zenkutsu Dachi)

Change position to Zenkutsu Dachi.

Delivers Kamae position for kicks

8) ↑↑ ↔ Nidan Mae Geri (Mae Geri Chudan and Mae Geri Jodan)

9) ↑ Mawashi Geri

Change position to Kiba Dachi

10) ↑↑ ↔ Yoko Geri Keage

11) ↑↑ ↔ Yoko Geri Kekomi

Kata

Heian Yondan

Kumite

Kihon Ippon Kumite – 1-time attack and defense.

Jodan X 1

Chudan X 1

Mae Geri X 1

Start from left-hand side or right-hand side (instructor's decision).

SENIORS - Counters must be a Zuki or Uchi.

*** BLUE BELT TO PURPLE BELT ***
(5th KYU TO 4th KYU)

Note: ↑ Advance moving

↓ Reverse moving

↔ Repeat the method

From Zenkutsu Dachi – Gedan Barai

1) ↑ Sanbon Zuki (Jodan, Chudan and Chudan)

2) ↓ Sanbon Gyaku Zuki (Chudan, Jodan and Chudan)

3) ↑ Age Uke and Gyaku Zuki

4) ↑ Soto Uke, Empi, Uraken (Empi as well as Uraken in Kiba Dachi)

5) ↑ Uchi Uke, Kizami Zuki and Gyaku Zuki

6) ↑↓ ↔ Spinning Gyaku Zuki

SHOTOKAN KARATE: EASIEST WAY TO GET BLACK BELT

Change position to Kokutsu Dachi

7) ↑ Shuto Uke (Nukite in Zenkutsu Dachi)

Change position to Zenkutsu Dachi

8) ↑ Ren Mae Geri (Kizami Mae Geri and Mae Geri)

9) ↑ Mawashi Geri

10) ↑↑ ↔ Nidan Mae Geri (Mae Geri Chudan as well as Mae Geri Jodan)

Change position to Kiba Dachi

11) ↑↑ ↔ Yoko Geri Keage

12) ↑↑ ↔ Yoko Geri Kekomi

Kata

Heian Godan

Kumite

Kihon Ippon Kumite – 1-time attack and defense.

Jodan X 1

Chudan X 1

Mae Geri X 1

Mawashi Geri X 1

Yoko Geri Kekomi X 1

Start from left-hand side or right-hand side (instructor's decision).

SENIORS - counters must be a Zuki or Uchi.

*** PURPLE BELT TO 3rd BROWN BELT ***
(4th KYU to 3rd KYU)

Note: ↑ Advance moving

↓ Reverse moving

↔ Repeat the method

From Zenkutsu Dachi – Gedan Barai

1) ↑ Sanbon Zuki (Jodan, Chudan and Chudan)

2) ↓ Sanbon Gyaku Zuki: (Chudan, Jodan and Chudan)

3) ↑ Age Uke and Gyaku Zuki

4) ↑ Soto Uke, Empi, Uraken (Empi as well as Uraken in Kiba Dachi)

5) ↑ Uchi Uke, Kizami Zuki and Gyaku Zuki

6) ↑↓ ↔ Spinning Gyaku Zuki

Change position to Kokutsu Dachi

7) ↑ Shuto Uke (Nukite in Zenkutsu Dachi)

Change position to Zenkutsu Dachi

8) ↑ Ren Mae Geri (Kizami Mae Geri and Mae Geri)

9) ↑ Mawashi Geri

10) ↑↑ ↔ Nidan Mae Geri (Mae Geri Chudan and Mae Geri Jodan)

Change position to Kiba Dachi

11) ↑↑ ↔ Yoko Geri Keage

12) ↑↑ ↔ Yoko Geri Kekomi

Kata

SHOTOKAN KARATE: EASIEST WAY TO GET BLACK BELT

Tekki Shodan

Kumite

Kihon Ippon Kumite:

Jodan x 2

Chudan x 2

Mae Geri x 2

Mawashi Geri x 2

Yoko Geri Kekomi x 2

Start from left-hand side or right-hand side (instructor's decision).

*** 3rd BROWN BELT to 2nd BROWN BELT***
(3rd KYU to 2nd KYU)

Note: ↑ Advance moving

↓ Reverse moving

↔ Repeat the method

From Zenkutsu Dachi – Gedan Barai

1) ↑ Sanbon Zuki (Jodan, Chudan and Chudan)

2) ↑ Sanbon Gyaku Zuki (Chudan, Jodan and Chudan)

3) ↓ Age Uke and Gyaku Zuki

4) ↑ Soto Uke, Empi and Uraken (Empi and Uraken in Kiba Dachi)

5) ↓ Uchi Uke, Kizami Zuki and Gyaku Zuki

6) ↑↓ ↔ Spinning Gyaku Zuki and Sanbon Zuki

Change position to Kokutsu Dachi

7) ↑↑↔ Spinning Shuto Uke

Change position to Zenkutsu Dachi

8) ↑ Mae Geri and Gyaku Zuki

9) ↑↑ ↔ Mawashi Geri, Uraken and Oi Zuki (venturing through with Oi Zuki)

Change position to Kiba Dachi

10) ↑↑ ↔ Yoko Geri Keage

11) ↑↑ ↔ Yoko Geri Kekomi

Change position to Zenkutsu Dachi

12) ↑↑ ↔ Ushiro Geri

Kata

Bassai Dai

Kumite

Jiyu Ippon Kumite:

Jodan X 2

Chudan X 2

Mae Geri X 2

Mawashi Geri X 2

Yoko Geri Kekomi X 2

Start from left-hand side or right-hand side (instructor's decision).

SHOTOKAN KARATE: EASIEST WAY TO GET BLACK BELT

*** 2nd BROWN BELT to 1st BROWN BELT ***
(2nd KYU to 1st KYU)

Note: ↑ Advance moving

↓ Reverse moving

↔ Repeat the method

Karate-ka to show every procedure multiple times.

Kihon

From Zenkutsu Dachi – Gedan Barai

1) ↑ Mae Geri and Oi Zuki (no progression through)

2) ↑ Mawashi Geri and Gyaku Zuki (no progress through)

3) ↑↑ ↔ Mae Geri, (step-over) Oi-Zuki and Gyaku Zuki

4) ↑↑ ↔ Mae Geri and Mawashi Geri (swap legs)

5) ↑ Kizami Yoko Geri Kekomi and Ushiro Geri

6) ↑ Shuto, Kizami Mae Geri and Nukite

Change position to Kiba Dachi

7) ↑↑ ↔ Yoko Geri Keage and Yoko Geri Kekomi (venturing over, kicking with the same leg)

Change position to Fudo Dachi

8) ↑↓ ↔ Fudo Dachi Oi Zuki

Kata

Shitei Kata (necessary Kata): Tekki Shodan

Sentei Kata (free decision Kata) from Bassai-Dai

SHOTOKAN KARATE: EASIEST WAY TO GET BLACK BELT

Kanku-Dai

Empi

Jion

Kumite

Jiyu Ippon Kumite – Free 1-time attack and block.

Jodan X 2

Chudan X 2

Mae Geri X 2

Mawashi Geri X 2

Yoko Geri Kekomi X 2

Ushiro Geri X 2

Kizami Zuki X 2

Gyaku Zuki X 2

Counters must be a Zuki in turn with Uchi.

Start from left-hand side or right-hand side (instructor's decision).

*** SHOTOKAN KARATE DAN GRADE EXAMINATIONS ***
*** SHODAN BLACK BELT OR 1st DAN ***
(1st KYU to 1st DAN)

Note: ↑ Advance moving

↓ Reverse moving

↔ Repeat the strategy

Karate-ka to show every method multiple times.

SHOTOKAN KARATE: EASIEST WAY TO GET BLACK BELT

Kihon

From Zenkutsu Dachi – Gedan Barai

1) ↑ Sanbon Zuki (Jodan, Chudan and Chudan)

2) ↑ Sanbon Gyaku Zuki (turning first Gyaku Zuki Chudan, Jodan and Chudan)

3) ↓ Age Uke, Tate Uraken and Gyaku Zuki (Age Uke, steep Uraken with the same arm)

4) ↑ Soto Uke, Empi in Kiba Dachi to one side, turning Uraken, Gyaku Zuki in Zenkutsu Dachi to frontside.

5) ↓ Uchi Uke, Kizami Zuki, Gyaku Zuki and Mawashi with Empi.

Change position to Kokutsu Dachi

6) ↑ Spinning Shuto Uke and Kizami Geri (Nukite in Zenkutsu Dachi)

Change position to Zenkutsu Dachi – Gedan Barai

Karate-ka to exhibit every system multiple times.

7) ↑↑ ↔ Mae Geri and Mawashi Geri with Gyaku Zuki.

8) ↑↑ ↔ Mae Geri, Yoko Geri, Keage and Gyaku Zuki.

Change position to Zenkutsu Dachi, confronting the Coach (Shomen Kamae)

9) ↑ Mae Geri and Mawashi Geri (equally leg to front)

10) ↑ Mawashi Geri and Kekomi Geri (equally leg to front)

Kata

Shitei Kata (necessary Kata): Examiner's decision from Heian 1 – 5

Tekki Shodan

SHOTOKAN KARATE: EASIEST WAY TO GET BLACK BELT

Sentei Kata (free decision Kata) from Bassai-Dai

Kanku-Dai

Empi

Jion

Kumite

Analyst's decision: Jiyu Ippon Kumite – Free 1-time attack and protection OR Jiyu Kumite – Free competing

Jodan X 2 Yoko Geri Kekomi X 2 times

Chudan X 2 and Ushiro Geri X 2 times

Mae Geri X 2 and Kizami Zuki X 2 times

Mawashi Geri X 2 and Gyaku Zuki X 2 times

Retaliate must be a Zuki and Uchi.

Start from left-hand side or right-hand side (instructor's decision).

*** REQUIREMENTS FOR A KYU GRADING IN SHOTOKAN KARATE ***

9th KYU to 8th KYU - **30 Nonstop classes.**

8th KYU to 7th KYU - **30 Nonstop classes.**

7th KYU to 6th KYU - **45 Nonstop classes.**

6th KYU to 1st KYU - **45 Nonstop classes.**

SHOTOKAN KARATE
COLOUR BELTS ORDER

The main thought for fitting the bill to endeavor a KYU evaluation is that the base measure of required persistent classes has been taken or not. A regular Karate class implies that you have been preparing persistently with no break in the middle of preparation. An authorized or approved evaluating authority will enable a student to pass a KYU grade in the Ninth KYU to Seventh KYU stages, if the student shows excellent capacity. The same applies to junior belt grades also. This choice is altogether at the disposal of the reviewing official. Dojos should conduct four KYU reviewing assessments every year. For hard-working and consistently preparing students, it should be reviewed by reviewing officials thrice a year only.

*** POINT SYSTEM IN SHOTOKAN KARATE ***

If a point structure is being utilized, the analyst may allocate 10 points each to Kihon, Kata, and Kumite that are as follows:

The author showing Jodan, Chudan, and Gedan point scoring area.

SHOTOKAN KARATE: EASIEST WAY TO GET BLACK BELT

A. FOR KIHON:

1. Lunge punch movement, 3 points.
2. Spirit and eye projection, 2 points.
3. Rising obstruction movement, 1 point.
4. Forearm obstruction movement, 1 point.
5. Knife-hand obstruction movement, 1 point.
6. Front kick movement, 1 point.
7. Sidekick movement, 1 point.

B. FOR KATA:

1. Correct arrangement of movements, 4 points.
2. Application of solidarity, productive compression, movement of the body and speed, 2 points.
3. Attitude, 2 points.
4. Spirit, KIAI, and eye projection, 1.5 points.
5. Embusen (a spot where Kata starts and ends), 0.5 points.

C. FOR KUMITE:

1. Fast, vivacious attack on offense, 2 points.
2. The Focus of attack on offense, 2 points.
3. Effective obstruction, 2 points.
4. Accurate and powerful counterattack, 2 points.
5. Smooth progress from obstruction to counterattack, 2 points.

*** SPECIFICATIONS OF SHOTOKAN KATA BASSAI DAI ***

Bassai (articulated as Patsai in Okinawan) is frequently known as "**To penetrate a fortress**," implying that one must show the power and spirit required to get through an adversary's stronghold. Bassai Dai is a Kata drilled in Shotokan Karate and is one of the many types of the Passai Kata. There are two Bassai Kata, Bassai Sho and Bassai Dai. "**SHO**" means "small," and it is taught after Bassai Dai. The word "**DAI**" signifies "big," portraying the Kata's more prominent movements, in opposition to its partner Bassai Sho. Bassai, Kanku, and Gojushiho are the three Shotokan Kata that each have two forms; a Sho rendition (little) and a Dai variant (huge). Most interpreters concur that Bassai can all the more precisely be interpreted as "To Extract from a Fortress." Bassai Dai is accepted to have been made by Sokon Matsumura. In the same way as other Shotokan Kata, Bassai Dai is practised in numerous Karate styles, having a few varieties. Bassai Dai is typically classed as a middle Kata and is commonly first taught to Karateka at third KYU. In some Shotokan organizations, it is executed as a reviewing Kata to the extent of 1st DAN (Black Belt). It is fascinating to take note that one of the most fundamental blocking strategies, Chudan-Soto-Uke, was first utilized in this Kata, and after that, it spread to other forms. Yama Zuki is also the part of Bassai Dai. Presently, the JKA has 42 Bassai Dai movements, but many Shotokan federations perform 62 movements for better understanding of the Katas. I have also performed 62 movements for the Bassai Dai Kata. So, lets have a look to understand Bassai Dai step-wise procedure with **high-resolution photos** for better knowledge and comprehension.

SHOTOKAN KARATE: EASIEST WAY TO GET BLACK BELT

*** STEPWISE PROCEDURE OF SHOTOKAN KATA BASSAI DAI ***

Take the Shizentai stance (Normal Position). **(STEP-1)**

Adjoin both the feet. Left hand will wrap around the right .st and left thumb will be put on top of right 30K (area between thumb and ﹨▱◸◮ 圀 ◯◮▱◮◮▨ **(STEP-2)**

Put both the hands-on left side, at the same time, lift the right leg up and forward. **(STEP-3)**

Perform augmented-forearm block (Morote Uchi Uke) in crossed leg stance (Kosa Dachi) and knee locked. **(STEP-4)**

SHOTOKAN KARATE: EASIEST WAY TO GET BLACK BELT

Turn 180-degree and put left hand below right-hand shoulder's base. **(STEP-5)**

Execute inside forearm block (Uchi Uke) by left hand. **(STEP-6)**

With the help of right arm, perform reverse inside forearm block (Gyaku Uchi Uke). **(STEP-7)**

Turn the body to 180-degree by lifting left arm upwards and stretch the right arm forward. **(STEP-8)**

SHOTOKAN KARATE: EASIEST WAY TO GET BLACK BELT

Execute right leg slightly right on taking reverse and with the help of left arm, execute reverse outside forearm block (Gyaku Soto Uke) and keep right hand near waist line. **(STEP-9)**

Right hand across stomach and left hand bent. **(STEP-10)**

Perform Uchi-Uke on the right side with right leg forward. **(STEP-11)**

Take turn 90-degree on the right and keep right hand parallel to the top of head. **(STEP-12)**

SHOTOKAN KARATE: EASIEST WAY TO GET BLACK BELT

Perform Soto-Uke by right arm. **(STEP-13)**

Left arm across stomach and perform Gyaku Uchi Uke by left arm. **(STEP-14)**

Take Shizentai stance and put both the hands on the right side. Put left hand's fist (facing down side) on right hand's fist. **(STEP-15)**

Slow movement by left hand with Tate Shuto **(STEP-16)**

SHOTOKAN KARATE: EASIEST WAY TO GET BLACK BELT

Execute Choku Zuki with the right arm. **(STEP-17)**

Move right arm on left chest side and keep left hand at waist level. **(STEP-18)**

Implement body to 90-degree on left side and perform Uchi Uke. **(STEP-19)**

Turn body to 90-degree on right side and perform Uchi Uke. **(STEP-20)**

Conduct right side Shuto Uke in Kokutsu Dachi stance. **(STEP-21)**

Perform Shuto Uke on left side in Kokutsu Dachi stance. **(STEP-22)**

Conduct right side Shuto Uke in Kokutsu Dachi stance. **(STEP-23)**

Put a step backward and perform left side Shuto Uke in Kokutsu Dachi stance. **(STEP-24)**

SHOTOKAN KARATE: EASIEST WAY TO GET BLACK BELT

Put right arm in Soto Uke position with palm down and hand open. Place left hand near right hand thumb base. **(STEP-25)**

Lift the right knee up to the waist level and keep both hands near chest area. **(STEP-26)**

Implement Fumikomi with a loud KIAI and put fists near chest. **(STEP-27)**

Step down with right leg and perform left side Shuto Uke in Kokutsu Dachi stance. **(STEP-28)**

SHOTOKAN KARATE: EASIEST WAY TO GET BLACK BELT

Play Right side Shuto Uke in Kokutsu Dachi stance. **(STEP-29)**

Straighten the legs, feet with no gap, little gap between the Knuckles and stop the 30⊕above the forehead. **(STEP-30)**

While pushing both arms forward and up, step with right leg. **(STEP-31)**

Perform small front step stance. **(STEP-32)**

SHOTOKAN KARATE: EASIEST WAY TO GET BLACK BELT

Perform right hand big front step punch. **(STEP-33)**

Perform Shuto with left hand and set right hand for a strike. **(STEP-34)**

Strike with Nukite and palm heel block. **(STEP-35)**

With slow motion (it takes four seconds to make a stance), right hand will go above head and left hand downwards. Legs get straightened. **(STEP-36)**

SHOTOKAN KARATE: EASIEST WAY TO GET BLACK BELT

Execute half-moon round by raising right leg up to the waist level and take right arm above the left shoulder. At the same time, on landing with right leg, strike with the right hand. Stand on left leg. **(STEP-37)**

Land the right leg with downward block (Gedan Barai) in horse stance (Kiba Dachi). **(STEP-38)**

Bring left arm below the right shoulder base with the palm facing down and right hand near left chest side. **(STEP-39)**

In slow motion (it takes four seconds), extend left arm into back hand block (Haishu Uke). **(STEP-40)**

SHOTOKAN KARATE: EASIEST WAY TO GET BLACK BELT

Kick Mikazuki Geri (Crescent Kick) through right leg while grabbing its feet by left hand. Total body weight and balance will be on the left leg. **(STEP-41)**

Land with round elbow strike (Mawashi Empi Uchi) in Kiba Dachi stance. Left hand will be on front side and at the same time parallel to the right hand. **(STEP-42)**

Perform right arm punches downwards and keep left arm at right hand forearm in Kiba Dachi stance. (1st sequence) **(STEP-43)**

Attack with left arm and put right hand fist at left hand forearm in Kiba Dachi stance. (2nd sequence) **(STEP-44)**

SHOTOKAN KARATE: EASIEST WAY TO GET BLACK BELT

Perform right arm punches downwards and keep left arm at right hand forearm in Kiba Dachi stance (3rd sequence). **(STEP-45)**

Pulling both hands-on left sides where right hand's 拳(facing downward) will be put on left hand's 拳 **(STEP-46)**

Perform U-stance (Yamazuki stance) for the first time. Turn body to 90-degree on right and left arm will be above the head. Both hand's fists will be facing each other. **(STEP-47)**

Slowly put right leg back and join with left leg. Both legs will be straight. Right hand's fist will be on left hand's fist, facing downwards. Position of both hands will be on right side. **(STEP-48)**

SHOTOKAN KARATE: EASIEST WAY TO GET BLACK BELT

Move left leg up and forward and keep both the hands-on right-hand side. Both hand's facing one another and left hand's will be facing downwards. **(STEP-49)**

Land with U-Punch (Yamazuki stance) for the 2nd time and both arms will be at equal distance from the body. Right hand will come over the head. **(STEP-50)**

Slowly pull left leg back and adjoin both the feet. Both hands will come on left side keeping right hand's fist (facing downwards) on left hand's fist. **(STEP-51)**

Move right leg up and forward. Both hands will be on left side. Right hand's fist (facing downwards) will be put on left hand's fist. **(STEP-52)**

Drive right leg forward and perform Yamazuki stance (U-block) for the third time. **(STEP-53)**

Rotate body with 270-degree where right hand is upward and left hand is downward. **(STEP-54)**

Sweeping the right arm across the body, apply a round (like numerical 6 putting horizontally) by the right hand. **(STEP-55)**

Extend left hand upwards and keep right hand downwards. left leg will be forwarded and both legs will be in a line. **(STEP-56)**

SHOTOKAN KARATE: EASIEST WAY TO GET BLACK BELT

Sweeping the left arm, perform hooking movement (like numerical 6 putting horizontally). Right leg will be forwarded and both legs will be in a line. **(STEP-57)**

Move body to 45-degree on right and perform right side Shuto-Uke in Kokutsu Dachi stance. **(STEP-58)**

Look 45-degree to the left side and put right leg 45-degree to the back side. Remain in right side Shoto-Uke in Kokutsu Dachi stance. **(STEP-59)**

Perform left side Shuto-Uke in Kokutsu Dachi stance with a loud **KIAI**. **(STEP-60)**

Again, come in YOI position. **(STEP-61)**

Take Shizentai or Normal Position. **(STEP-62)**

*** SHOTOKAN KARATE TERMINOLOGY ***

Ai-Uchi: Indicating concurrent attacks; hence, no score.

Aka No Kachi / Shiro No Kachi: Signifying red or white is the champion, respectively.

Aka: Red contender.

Ao: Blue contender.

Ashi-Barai: Foot sweep.

Ato Shibaraku: Alerting the contenders that there are just 30 seconds left in the match.

Awasete Ippon: To demonstrate that score included makes a full point.

Budo: Way of combat.

Bunkai: Application (interpretation) of Kata techniques.

Chui: A proper admonition.

Dachi: Stance.

Do: Means *way* or *path*. It is the way for the ultimate perfection of human character.

Dojo: Training hall.

Embusen: Start and end spot line in a Kata.

Fumikomi-Waza: Stepping systems.

Geri: Kick (Used after the type of kick, i.e., Mae Geri).

Gi: A Karate uniform.

Godo-Kata: Group structure in which a gathering of students play out the equivalent Kata as one;

Gohon Kumite: Five-step sparring.

Hai: Used for affirmation, as in 'yes' or 'okay.' It is also used to give commands, as in 'Okay', 'let's go', or 'lineup'.

Hajime: Begin or Start or Go.

Hansoku: Disqualifying a contender from the match.

Hantei: Indicating choice time.

Hayai: Indicating that one attack is quicker than the other (in the trade of blows).

Hayaku: Move with speed.

Hikiwake: Indicating a draw.

Ippon Kumite: One-step sparring.

Ippon: To show a full point (a blow with the possibility to wrap up).

Jiyu-Ippon-Kumite: Semi-free competing.

Jiyu-Kumite: Free-form fighting.

Jogai: Indicating out of the zone.

Kamae: Posture.

Kamaete: A command to move into a stance, ready for action.

Karate: Empty Hands.

Karate-do: The Way of Karate.

Karategi: A Karate uniform.

Karateka: Practitioner of Karate.

Karuku: A command to move lightly, but with correct motion.

Kata: It is a form or formal exercise. There are two significant arrangements of Kata in preparing:

Kata-No-Keiko: Informal practice.

Keikoku: Cautioning either of the contenders.

Keri Waza: Kicking Techniques.

Ki: Vital force or mental energy.

Kiai: A sharp sound made at the moment of *kime* to aid in the tensing of body muscles and focusing of the mind for a more effective *kime*.

Kihon Kumite: Basic sparring.

Kihon: Fundamentals/Basics.

Kihon-Ippon-Kumite: One-step fighting.

Kihon-No-Keiko: Practice in fundamental methods.

Kiken: To show a withdrawal of contender/contenders.

Kime: Focus. It can signify "power," portraying the prompt straining at the right time during a technique.

Kiots Uke: Prepare for action.

Kogeki: To attack.

Kohai: A junior member of the dojo.

Kojin-Kata: A structure performed alone by an individual student.

Kumite: Competing.

Kumite-No-Keiko: Practice in sparring.

Kyu: Rank.

Ma-Ai: Distance. The right distance between two rivals.

Mae Ni: Push ahead.

Makiwara: A punching board that is padded and is struck forcefully to develop focusing on body strength.

Mawatte: Turn around.

Mizu-No-Kokoro: Mind like water.

Modotte: Come back to the first position.

Mokuso: Quiet thought or meditation. Mokuso is to accomplish mental and physical peacefulness.

Moto-No-Ichi: Telling competitor(s) to restore the beginning positions, i.e., the line.

Mubobi: Indicating non-guarding.

Mukai Ate: Face one another.

Nage-Waza: Throwing techniques.

Nakai: Competitors to enter the tatami. These are not utilized regularly in rivalry now.

Naotte: At ease or relax.

Narande: Lineup.

Nukite-Masu: Indicating an attack missed the objective.

Obi: Belt.

Onegai Shimasu: I commend you to train me.

Osu: Yes, I am with you with full spirit.

Otagai-Ni-Rei: Bow to one another.

Rei Bow: Different terms utilized with Rei.

Rei: Bow.

Renzoku-Waza: To demonstrate a mixed system.

Ryu: School or style.

Sai Shiai: Indicating a rematch.

Sakidori: Indicating an "unexpected demise" coordinates, in a second rematch circumstance, that is, the first contender to score will win the match.

Sanbon Kumite: Three-step sparring.

Seiretsu: Line up in a precise design.

Seiretsu: Line up orderly.

Seiza: The conventional Japanese strategy for sitting on the floor with the knees bowed and the legs under the body.

Sempai: A senior individual in a school or association.

Sensei: Teacher. The term might be applied to any individual who aides or trains another, for example, a specialist or legal advisor. Sensei signifies, "one who has gone previously."

Sensei-Ni-Rei: Bow to the instructor.

Shihan: Master (Calling with their title is prohibited).

Shipa Ni Rei: Bow to referees and judges. It is not done at many competitions now.

Shiro: White.

Shobu Hajime: Beginning the match.

Shomen Ni Rei: Asking contenders to bow to the front.

Shomen: Front. In the dojo, the Shomen is the front divider where a photo of the school's author is placed.

Shomen-Ni-Rei: Bow to the front.

Shotokan: Place of Shoto.

Shugo: Indicating assembling a conference between the corner judges and focus referees.

Suki: Opening.

Tai-Sabaki: Body shifting.

Tatte: Stand up.

Torimasen: Indicating no point is to be granted.

Tsuki (Zuki): Strike where the forearm is going in the direction of the fist.

Tsuki Waza: Punching systems.

Tsuki-No-Kokoro: Mind like the moon.

Tsuyoku: Execute healthy, fast techniques.

Tsuzukete Hajime: To restart the match.

Tsuzukete: Telling the contenders to "battle on" (proceed) if one of the two quits during the match.

Uchi: To hit where the forearm is not going in the line of the fist.

Uchi-Waza: Striking techniques.

Uke: To receive or Block.

Ukete-Masu: Indicating that an attack was blocked.

Undo: Exercises or equipments.

Ushiro Ni: Move backwards.

Waza: Techniques.

Waza-Ari: To demonstrate a half-point.

Yame: To stop a match.

Yasume: Relax.

Yoi: Be ready.

Yori-Ashi: Sliding the feet.

Yowai: Indicating that an attack was too feeble to even think about scoring.

Yowaku: Move softly.

Yukkuri: Move more slowly.

Zanshin: Poise and control; focus your mind.

*** TWENTY PRINCIPLES OF SHOTOKAN KARATE ***
(JAPANESE TO ENGLISH VERSION)

1. Karate-do wa rei ni hajimari, rei ni owarru koto wo wasurruna.

Karate starts and finishes with politeness.

2. Karate ni sente naashi.

There is no first attack in Karate.

3. Karate wa gi no tassuke.

Karate helps to equity.

4. Mazu jikko wo shire, shikoshitte tao wo shire.

Know yourself first, before you know others.

5. Gijuttsu yori shinjutsu.

Soul before method.

6. Kokoro wa hanattan koto wo yosu.

Be prepared to free your brain.

7. Wazawai wa getai ni shozzu.

Mishaps originate from sluggishness.

8. Dojo nomino Karate to ommou na.

Karate preparation goes past the dojo.

9. Karate no shogyo wa isho dearu.

You will continuously learn in Karate.

10. Arai-yurru mono wo Karate-ka seyo, soko ni myo-mi ari.

Apply Karate to everything. In that lies its excellence.

11. Karate wa yu no goto shi taezu nattsudo wo attaezareba moto no mizu ni kaeru.

Karate resembles bubbling water. If not given warmth, it will go cold.

12. Katsu kangae wa mottsu naa makenu kangae wa hittsuyo.

Try not to consider winning. Instead, I believe that you should never lose.

13. Tekki ni yote tenka seyo.

Change, as indicated by your adversary.

14. Tatakai wa kyo-jittsu no soju ikan ni ari.

It is merely in the center of the world.

15. Hito no te aashi wo ken to omoe.

Consider hands and feet to be swords.

16. Danshi mon wo izureba hyakuman no teki ari.

At the juncture when you step outside your entryway, you face a million adversaries.

17. Kamae wa shoshinasha ni atto wa shizentai.

Fixed positions are for apprentices: later, one usually moves.

18. Kata wa taadashiku jissen wa bettsu mono.

Kata practice is a different thing; a genuine battle is something else.

19. Chikara no kyojaaku, karaada no shinshukoo, waza no kankyu wo wasaruna.

Hard and delicate, pressure and unwinding, snappy and moderate, all associated in the strategy.

20. Tsune ni shinen kufu seyo.

Consider approaches to apply these statutes consistently.

*** SHARING RATIO OF BODY WEIGHT IN SHOTOKAN KARATE ***

(BETWEEN THE FRONT LEG AND THE BACK LEG)

(NEKO-ASHI-DACHI) **=2:8**

(ZENKUTSU-DACHI) **=6:4**

(KOKUTSU-DACHI) **=3:7**

(FUDO-DACHI) **=5:5**

(KIBA-DACHI) **=5:5**

SHOTOKAN KARATE: EASIEST WAY TO GET BLACK BELT

*** TARGET AREAS IN SHOTOKAN KARATE ***

You should be exact. You can't directly go out there and start whopping anyplace you want on your adversary's body and score a point. You can score just on these particular targets:

1. The head.
2. The face.
3. The neck.
4. The chest.
5. The midriff.
6. The sides of the body.
7. The back.

*** HANDS, FEET AND FISTS GLOSSARY IN SHOTOKAN KARATE ***

Empi: Elbow.

Haito: Edge hand.

Ippon ken: One-knuckle clench hand.

Koshi: Pod of foot.

Shuto: Blade's hand.

Teisho: Palm heel.

Tettsui: Base clench hand.

Uraken: Back clench hand.

Haisoku: Instep.

Hittsui: Knee.

Kakato: Heel.

Seiken: Fore-clench hand.

Sokuto: Foot edge.

Teisoku: Bottom of a foot.

Ude: Lower arm.

Yonhon-Nukite: Lance hand.

*** COUNTINGS IN SHOTOKAN KARATE ***

Ichi: One
Ni: Two
San: Three
Shi: Four
Go: five
Roku: Six

SHOTOKAN KARATE: EASIEST WAY TO GET BLACK BELT

Shichi: Seven **Hachi:** Eight **Ku:** Nine

Ju: Ten **NiJu:** Twenty **Ippon:** First

*** DIRECTIONS IN SHOTOKAN KARATE ***

Chudan: Neck to Belt level. **Gedan:** Below the belt level.

Gyaku: Reverse. **Hidari:** Left. **Jodan:** Head high-level.

Mae: Front. **Mawashi:** Round. **Migi:** Right.

Soto: Outer. **Uchi:** Inner. **Ushiro:** Back. **Yoko:** Side.

*** BLOCKS (UKE) IN SHOTOKAN KARATE ***

Age Uke: Rising obstruction.

Empi Uke (Hiji Uke): Elbow obstruction.

Gedan Uke: Down Obstruction.

Haishu Uke: Back-hand obstruction.

Juji Uke: X Obstruction.

Manji Uke: Vortex Block.

Morote Uke: Augmented Obstruction.

Soto Ude Uke: Outside forearm obstruction.

Tate Shuto Uke: Vertical blade hand obstruction.

*** KICKS (GERI) IN SHOTOKAN KARATE ***

Fumikomi Geri: Stamp kick.

Hiza Geri: Knee kick/strike.

Mae Geri Keage: Front snap kick.

Mawashi Geri: Roundhouse kick.

Nidan Geri: Twofold kick.

Soto Mikazuki Geri: Outside sickle kick.

Tobi Geri: Flying kick.

Uchi Mikazuki Geri: Inside sickle kick.

Ushiro Geri: Back push kick.

Ushiro Mawashi Geri: Reverse roundhouse kick.

Yoko Geri Kekomi: Side push kick.

*** PUNCHES (ZUKI) IN SHOTOKAN KARATE ***

Age Zuki: Rising punch.

Choku Zuki: Straight punch.

Gedan Zuki: Down punch.

Gyaku Zuki: Reverse punch.

Ippon Ken Zuki: One-knuckle clench hands punch (Hangetsu).

Kagi Zuki: Hook punch.

Mawashi-Zuki: Round punch.

SHOTOKAN KARATE: EASIEST WAY TO GET BLACK BELT

Morote Zuki: Parallel punch.

Nukite-Zuki: Lance hand push.

Oi Gyaku Zuki: Lunging reverse punch.

Oi-Zuki: Jump punch.

Otoshi Zuki: Dropping punch (Empi).

Ren Zuki: Double punch.

Sanbon Zuki: Triple punch.

Seiken-Choku-Zuki: Fore-clench hand straight punch.

Ura Zuki: Close punch.

Yame Zuki: Wide "U" punch, resembles like Mountain.

*** STRIKES (UCHI) IN SHOTOKAN KARATE ***

Empi Uchi: Elbow Strike.

Nukite Uchi: Spear Hand Strike.

Shuto Uchi: Knife Hand Strike.

Tate Empi Uchi: Upward Elbow Strike.

Teisho Uchi: Palm Heel Strike.

Uraken Uchi: Back fist Strike.

*** INDEX ***

Age Uke: 73

Chudan Uchi Uke: 78

Empi Uchi: 79

Fumikomi Geri: 81

Gedan Barai: 62

Gedan Uke: 168

Gohon Kumite: 125

Gyaku Zuki: 60

Hachiji Dachi: 106

Haishu Uke: 85

SHOTOKAN KARATE: EASIEST WAY TO GET BLACK BELT

Haisoku: 167	Hajime: 159
Hangetsu Dachi: 107	Hayaku: 159
Heiko Dachi: 105	Heisoku Dachi: 82
Hiza Geri: 59	Iaigoshi Dachi: 102
Ippon Kumite: 107	Jiyu Ippon Kumite: 64
Jodan Juji Uke: 112	Jodan Mae Geri: 69
Juji Uke: 76	Kakiwake Uke: 84
Kata Hiza Dachi: 100	Kiba Dachi: 108
Kizami Zuki: 62	Kokutsu Dachi: 68
Kosa Dachi: 75	Mae Geri: 80
Mae Keage Geri: 94	Mawashi Geri: 74
Mikazuki Geri: 111	Morote Uke: 83
Morote Ura Zuki: 104	Morote Yoko Zuki: 61
Morote Zuki Jodan: 61	Musubi Dachi: 105
Neko Ashi Dachi: 72	Nidan Geri: 56
Nukite Uchi: 108	Oi Zuki: 101
Osae Uke: 67	Renoji Dachi: 63
Sagi Ashi Dachi: 88	Sanbon Kumite: 162
Sanchin Dachi: 87	Seiken Zuki: 92
Seiken-Choku-Zuki: 170	Shiko Dachi: 69
Shuto Uchi: 109	Shuto Uke: 57
Sochin Dachi: 110	Sokume: 93

SHOTOKAN KARATE: EASIEST WAY TO GET BLACK BELT

Sokuto: 167	Soto Uke: 58
Sukui Uke: 63	Tate Empi Uchi: 96
Tate Shuto Uke: 99	Tate Uraken Uchi: 70
Teiji Dachi: 106	Teisho Awase Uke: 98
Teisho Uchi: 103	Tettsui: 167
Tettsui Uchi: 97	Tsuru Ashi Dachi: 89
Uchi Otoshi Uke: 71	Uchi Uke Gedan Barai: 95
Uchi Uke: 57	Ura Zuki: 91
Uraken Uchi: 60	Ushiro Geri: 77
Yama Zuki: 65	Yoi Dachi: 66
Yoko Empi: 90	Yoko Geri Keage: 59
Yoko Geri Kekomi: 58	Yoko Geri: 55
Yoko Tobi Geri: 56	Zenkutsu Dachi: 86

*** BIBLIOGRAPHY ***

Abernethy, Iain, *Bunkai Jutsu, Volume 1, the Pinan/Heian Series*, DVD 120 minutes, Summersdale, 2006.

Abernethy, Iain, *Combat Drills*, DVD 70 minutes, Summersdale, 2007.

Abernethy, Iain, *Karate's Grappling Methods*, NETH Publishing in association with Summersdale Publishers LTD, England, 2000.

Abernethy, Iain, *Karate's Joint Locks*, Volume 3, DVD 60 minutes, 2005.

Abernethy, Iain, *Kata-Based Sparring*, DVD 70 minutes, Summersdale 2006.

SHOTOKAN KARATE: EASIEST WAY TO GET BLACK BELT

Adams, Brian, *The Medical Implications of Karate Blows*, A.S. Barnes & Co., 1969.

Alexander, George, *An Analysis of Medieval Japanese Warrior Culture and Samurai Thought as Applied to the Strategy and Dynamics of Japan's Twentieth Century Era of Warfare*, doctoral dissertation, Western Pacific University, 2001.

Alexander, George, *Hakutsuru, Secret of the White Crane*, Yamazato Videos, 2002.

Alexander, George, *Okinawa, Island of Karate*, Yamazato Publications, 1991.

Anonymous, *Karate-Do Kata*, Volumes 1 and 2, Japan Karate Association, 1994.

Appleman, Roy, et al, *United States Army in World War II, The War in the Pacific, Okinawa: The Last Battle*, Center of Military History, United States Army, Washington, D. C., 2000.

Ayoob, *The Truth about Self-Protection*, Police Bookshelf, 1985.

Bennett, Tony, *Early Japanese Images*, Tuttle, 1996.

Bishop, Mark, *Okinawan Karate, Teachers, Styles and Secret Techniques*, Tuttle, 1999.

Bruce Clayton. *Shotokan's Secret: The Hidden Truth Behind Karate's Fighting Origins*, ISBN 978-0897501880

CROFT, A.: Shotokan Karate. Ramsbury 2001.

ENOEDA, K.: Shotokan Karate 10th Kyu to 6th Kyu. London 1996.

ENOEDA, K.: Shotokan Karate 5th Kyu to Black Belt. London 1996.

ENOEDA, K.: Shotokan Karate Advanced Kata Vol. 1-3. Norwich 1983-86.

FUNAKOSHI, G.: Karate-do Kyohan. Tokio 1978.

Gichin Funakoshi. *Karate-do Kyohan: The Master Text*, ISBN 978-1568364827

Gichin Funakoshi. *Karate-do Nyumon: The Master Introductory Text*. ISBN 978-4770018915

GRUPP, J.: Shotokan Karate KATA Vol. 1. Oxford 2002.

GRUPP, J.: Shotokan Karate. Kihon-Kumite-Kata. Oxford 2002.

GURSHARAN, S.: Advanced Shotokan Karate Handbook. Bedford 1997.

HABERSETZER, R.: Shotokan Kata, Karate-Do Tome 1. Paris 1992.

Harry Cook. *Shotokan Karate: A Precise History*.

HASSELL, R.G.: Shotokan Karate: Its History and Evolution. St. Louis 1998.

HEALY, K.: A Step-by-step Guide to Shotokan Karate. London 2000.

John Sells. *Unante: The Secrets of Karate* (Panchita S. Hawley, 2nd ed. 2000), ISBN 0-910704-96-1

Marius Podeanu. Best Embusen: Shotokan.

Masatoshi Nakayama. *Dynamic Karate*, ISBN 978-1568364131

MILON, M.: Apprenez vos Katas de Base du Karaté Shotokan. Paris 1997.

NAKAYAMA, M.: Best Karate. Band 9-11. Tokio, New York, London 1989.

NAKAYAMA, M.: Karate-Do. Dynamic Karate. Sprendlingen 1972.

NISHIJAMA, H. & BROWN, R. C., Karate. Lauda 2001.

Randall G. Hassell and Edmond Otis. "The Complete Idiot's Guide to Karate". (Penguin Group (USA), 2000), ISBN 978-0028638324

Randall G. Hassell. *Shotokan Karate: Its History and Evolution* (Damashi, 1984. ISBN 0-911921-05-2.

REILLY, R.L.: The Secrets of Shotokan Karate. Boston 2000.

Rob Redmond. Kata: The Folk Dances of Shotokan.

SCHLATT: Shotokan No Hyakkajiten. Lauda 1995.

SCHMEISSER, E.: Bunkai. Secrets of Karate Kata, Volume 1: The Tekki Series. Missouri 2000.

SUGIYAMA, S.: 25 Shoto-Kan Kata. Chicago 2000.

Teruyuki Okazaki. *Perfection of Character: Guiding Principles for the Martial arts & Everyday Life,* ISBN 978-0978576325

TRIMBLE, A. & MORRIS, V.: Karate Kata Applications. London 1995.

V. WEENEN, J.: Advanced Shotokan Karate Kata. Wollaston 1987.

WICHMANN, W.D.: Kata 1-3. Niedernhausen 1985, 1986, 1990.

WORLD KARATE FEDERATION, WKF: Karatedo Kata Model, Shiteikata. Tokio 2001.

*The said photograph has been taken from https://2022.europeankaratefederation.net/ and is being used as part of fair use. The copyrights and other intellectual rights of the said photograph belong to the respective right owners.

www.ingramcontent.com/pod-product-compliance
Lightning Source LLC
LaVergne TN
LVHW070530070526
838199LV00075B/6751